Antiracism: A Critique

Antiracism: A Critique

JOHN SOLOMOS

polity

First published in 2025 by Polity Press

Polity Press
65 Bridge Street
Cambridge CB2 1UR, UK

Polity Press
111 River Street
Hoboken, NJ 07030, USA

ISBN-13: 978-1-5095-5621-2
ISBN-13: 978-1-5095-5622-9 (pb)

A catalogue record for this book is available from the British Library.

Library of Congress Control Number: 2024937985

Typeset in 11 on 14pt Warnock Pro
by Cheshire Typesetting Ltd, Cuddington, Cheshire
Printed and bound in Great Britain by CPI Group (UK) Ltd, Croydon

The publisher has used its best endeavours to ensure that the URLs for external websites referred to in this book are correct and active at the time of going to press. However, the publisher has no responsibility for the websites and can make no guarantee that a site will remain live or that the content is or will remain appropriate.

Every effort has been made to trace all copyright holders, but if any have been overlooked the publisher will be pleased to include any necessary credits in any subsequent reprint or edition.

For further information on Polity, visit our website:
politybooks.com

Contents

Preface

The idea for this book came to me at the time when there were mobilizations around the symbol of Black Lives Matter in 2014, and then again in 2020. Alongside broader conversations about the continuing significance of racialized inequalities, decolonization of the curriculum in fields such as education, and ongoing efforts to develop policies to deal with the everyday realities of cultural, religious and other differences in our societies, these mobilizations and protests raised the question of how we can develop a better understanding both of the changing forms of racism in the world around us and of the efforts to develop strategies informed by ideas and values that sought to overcome racism. The latter are often talked about under the generic term of *antiracism*. Give this background, it seemed important to me to place the question of antiracism squarely on the agenda in terms of both research and scholarly conversations, but also to explore the linkages between these conversations and policy and political debates.

This book takes as its starting point the argument that we need to address the question of antiracism more centrally in scholarship and research about race and racism in contemporary societies. It has grown out of a concern to engage with the question of how we can address the challenges we face in developing a critical analysis of the development of antiracist strategies and standpoints over the past few decades, and their implications for the future. Although we have some accounts of both of these issues, there are notable gaps in our historical understanding as well as the analysis of the current situation. This book is therefore an intervention into current debates that have emerged, particularly in recent times, about what kind of antiracist strategies we need in the present in order to address racialized inequalities and racism. Like much research in sociology, and the social sciences more generally, it is driven by curiosity and by an engagement with ongoing conversations in the society around us. In this case, I am curious to know more about the silences on antiracism and what can be done to encourage more conversations about this important issue.

In engaging in these ongoing conversations, I am aware that there is a need to hear different voices on how we can imagine antiracist futures in the world around us, and so this book is offered as a way to push some key aspects of current scholarly and policy debates forwards. Indeed, part of the point of writing this book is to encourage more research and scholarly reflection on antiracism as both a historical and contemporary phenomenon. Even as the book is being written, it is clear that the issues it addresses are constantly evolving and changing, and no doubt different perspectives from the one outlined here will be offered in the coming period. Questions about racism and antiracism are increasingly at the heart of political controversies across the globe, as has become evident over the past decade in the US, the UK, Europe, Brazil, and more generally across the globe. Debates about antiracism are very much part of the culture wars going on around us at the present time.

In writing this book, I have accumulated a number of debts to both individuals and institutions that I would like to acknowledge. First of all, I would like to thank my family, particularly Christine, Nikolas and Daniel, who have helped me maintain a sense of perspective as I worked on this book, even when it meant spending too much time in the study. Second, my long-standing collaboration with Martin Bulmer in editing the journal *Ethnic and Racial Studies* together, from 1995 to 2020, was another important influence on my work, including that which led to this book. I am grateful to Martin for his generosity of spirit and his constant encouragement to pursue my interests. Third, it is also important for me that I have been able to discuss many of the ideas that have coalesced into this book with various generations of students at Birkbeck; Southampton; City, University of London; and Warwick. In trying to teach them, I learned myself along the way, just as I hope they did. I am grateful for the opportunity they gave me to try out some of the ideas and arguments that have found their way into this book. Finally, for help of various kinds along the way, I would also like to acknowledge the support of numerous friends and colleagues, including Claire Alexander, Les Back, Manuela Bojadžijev, Milena Chimienti, Adrian Favell, Nicholas Gane, Paul Gilroy, Clive Harris, Michael Keith, Caroline Knowles, Marco Martiniello, Nasar Meer, Ali Meghji, Karim Murji, Steve Pile, Liza Schuster, Miri Song, Brett St Louis, Satnam Virdee, Aaron Winter and Eda Yazici. I am blessed to count on their collegial support and interest in talking through issues of common concern to all of us. Colleagues in the Department of Sociology at the University of Warwick have provided a supportive base for me for over a decade, and I am grateful for their ongoing support and encouragement. Warwick is in many ways a unique university and I have benefitted in many ways from being part of it. It is also important to acknowledge the support of my publisher at Polity, Jonathan Skerrett, who has been very helpful and enthusiastic at all stages of the development of this project, even when I was late.

During the writing of this book, I have enjoyed my walks and meditations around Crouch End, Parkland Walk, Highgate Wood, Queens Wood, Hampstead, Alexandra Park and Priory

Park, and other parts of North London. Not only do they give me the opportunity to enjoy the natural soundscapes as well as my musical ones, but they help to keep me relaxed and focused on thinking through some of the key arguments outlined in this book. During my walks, I was blessed to be able to listen to the music of Rhiannon Giddens, Nina Simone, Sam Cooke, Horace Andy and so many other musicians whose music helped me reflect on what I was trying to say in this book. I am also blessed to be a supporter of West Bromwich Albion, and my trips to watch them all over the country helped by providing both a distraction and enjoyment in equal measure. Along with travelling companions from the London Baggies, I have enjoyed a number of memorable, and sometimes painful, trips to watch our storied and beloved team. For me, WBA have been and will always remain more than a football team.

John Solomos
Crouch End, London

1

Rethinking Antiracism

Antiracism has been and remains relatively neglected in scholarly and research agendas, although it is often referred to in public discussions about such topics as racial disadvantage, immigration, education, policing and related policy issues. This relative neglect is not easy to explain in the current intellectual climate. Given the rapid expansion of research and teaching on questions about race and racism since the end of the twentieth century, we now have large and expanding bodies of scholarship on various facets of racism in contemporary societies, as well as increasing amounts of historical research that explores the changing role of race and racism in modern societies (Andersen and Collins 2020; Golash-Boza 2016; Solomos 2020). Whatever the merits of the key strands of scholarship and research on racism that have become entrenched in much of higher education and beyond over the past few decades, the end result of the expanding bodies of work that have been produced over this period is that we now have a more rounded and nuanced understanding of how racisms have evolved and impacted on the world around us over the past few centuries. In particular, we now have important bodies of research and scholarship on key facets of the workings of race and racism in shaping social and political relations in contemporary societies. There is also a wide range of studies of both national trends and developments as well as some comparative accounts of the role of race and racism both historically and in the present. There has also been a rapid expansion of specialized journals focusing on race and racism, as well as increasing coverage of these issues in mainstream social science journals

Yet, with a few notable exceptions, relatively little attention has been given to critical accounts of antiracism, its origins and impact both on historical processes and on contemporary societies (Bonnett 2000; van Dijk 2021; Zamalin 2019). There are a number of accounts of antiracism that date back to the 1990s and early 2000s, and they provide an important resource in trying to trace the histories of antiracism at the end of the twentieth century, including the important mobilizations that took place against the growth of neo-fascist and other extreme right political movements and ideologies (Anthias and Lloyd 2002; Lloyd 1998; Twine and Blee 2001). But these accounts do not cover the developments over the past three decades or provide a guide to the ideological and policy shifts that we have seen over this period.

This lack of attention to antiracism as a social and political phenomenon has meant that relatively little historical or contemporary scholarship has explored in any detail the national, local and community-level mobilizations of antiracist movements and organizations. There have been some important studies of the evolution and changing role of antiracist movements in European societies as well as in North America (Bakan and Dua 2014; Fella and Ruzza 2013), but again there is a clear need for more detailed accounts of these movements and mobilizations and their complex histories.

In order to redress this relative neglect of antiracism in dominant research agendas, there is a need to rethink our scholarly and policy frameworks through a critical intervention framed around the need for a more sustained conversation about antiracism and its positioning in wider debates about race and racism in the world around us. It may seem evident that by studying racisms in the past and the present we can also address questions about what can be done to tackle their impact on the social, political and cultural institutions of our societies. Yet, as will be argued throughout this book, such taken-for-granted assumptions have tended to undervalue the importance of both empirical and conceptual work on the dynamics of antiracist interventions, both historically and in the present. It remains important, therefore, to develop new critical bodies of scholarship and research that address the complex question of what kinds of antiracist strategies and agendas are necessary, both generally and to meet the specific situations in different parts of the globe. This is particularly important at a time when we are witnessing the evolution and expression of new forms of racism, including opposition to migration and refugee movement, in the public sphere as well as in public political and social discourses across a wide range of societies.

It is in this volatile environment that antiracism has become the target of ideological attacks from both neo-conservative and right-wing ideologues in the contemporary period. Such attacks have sought to dismiss antiracism as an ideology that represents a threat to Western values and as a danger both to social cohesion and to the interests of the very minorities that antiracism seeks to protect and serve. While it is difficult to say that these attacks from the right speak with one voice (see, for example, Ehsan 2023; McWhorter 2021), they do provide a body of writing that needs to be addressed if we are going to be able to develop a more open scholarly and policy debate about the possibilities of developing a radical antiracism that can address the realities of racism and racial injustice in the current environment.

At the same time, part of my concern in writing this book has been to push back against the tendency, at least in scholarly and research circles, to be dismissive of the possibilities of creating a space for radical antiracist politics in contemporary societies. This is evident in a growing trend for commentators from the left to put a strong emphasis on the relative failures of antiracist policies and to argue that little has changed as a result of policies and political interventions over the past few decades that have sought to tackle racial inequalities and divisions. Indeed, some commentators seem to be arguing, rhetorically at least, that little has changed over the past centuries, let alone the past few decades (Kundnani 2023; Shafi and Nagdee 2022; Warmington 2024). This has been evident both in the public debates about mobilizations under the banner of Black Lives Matter in the US and globally, and in the controversies around immigration, race and multiculturalism that are raging in a wide range of societies. Such arguments rhetorically point to the permanence of racism in terms of structures and institutions, and in doing this they seek to highlight the limited nature of the changes that we have seen in the current conjuncture. While it is important to remain critical of what policies and mobilizations have been able to achieve in recent times, there are also evident failings in accounts that argue that little or no change has been achieved in the struggles against racism and racialized inequalities.

It is important to engage more fully with two key questions that are urgent in the contemporary environment. First, there is the question of what can be done to challenge the role of racism and racial inequalities in the societies that we live in today, rather than presuming that the only change possible is through the creation of a wholly new society at some point in the future. Second, it is also important to explore how we can develop strategies for tackling barriers to radical change both in public institutions and in the private sectors, including key financial, legal and cultural industries both nationally and globally. Both of these questions need to be addressed by more detailed research into the workings of antiracism in specific societies and in institutions if we are going to be able to develop a critical antiracism that can meet the challenges that we face in the world around us today.

The rest of this chapter will lay out some of the key arguments that frame the book as a whole. We begin by placing antiracism within the broader bodies of historical and contemporary research into racism and antiracism. This leads us into an engagement with the question about why we have seen increased interest in thinking beyond race, and the broader social and political context that has helped to shape the current discussion about the shifting understandings of antiracism in the present. The chapter concludes by providing a synoptic overview of the chapters that follow.

Before moving on to a detailed analysis of the challenges outlined above, I want to take the opportunity in the rest of this chapter to discuss the histories and evolving forms of antiracism. In doing so, we shall also need to touch on the changing histories and expressions of racism but, given the focus of this book, we shall prioritize the processes that have helped to shape the various forms of antiracism. In developing this account, our main concern will be to lay the foundations for the more detailed analysis of antiracisms in the present. But we shall begin with setting out the historical context to contemporary antiracisms.

Histories and the present

What is today called antiracism can be traced back historically through the centuries that witnessed the emergence of ideas about race and racism. A number of overviews of antiracism, both as a generalized phenomenon across different societies and as one specific to national histories, have highlighted the long history of ideas and movements that have sought to challenge racism and the embedded structures of racial domination and oppression (van Dijk 2021; Zamalin 2019). Although much of the ideological infrastructure of antiracism as a set of ideas can be traced to the period after the Holocaust and the Second World War, there are indeed much longer histories of resistance to and opposition to racism, slavery and colonial violence and domination. These histories have been carefully researched by historians and by scholars in the humanities and social sciences, particularly as a result of the growing number of scholars who have sought to give voice to the everyday forms of resistance to slavery and bondage, opposition to the violence and destruction of colonial regimes and the politics of emancipation and empowerment in the aftermath of plantation slavery (Dubois 2012; Zoellner 2020). Much of this scholarship has been carried out over the past few decades and it has helped us to develop a more nuanced and detailed understanding of these histories of resistance to racism.

The histories of opposition and resistance to racism, slavery and colonialism have not always featured in the mainstream historical scholarship, whether in relation to the Americas, Europe or other parts of the globe. Indeed, it can be argued that in many ways we have seen ongoing processes of erasure, forgetting and silence about these histories over an extended period. The work of scholars such as W. E. B. Du Bois among others did seek to make these connections more central, but until the 1960s and 1970s such voices remained marginal to the core disciplinary and cross-disciplinary research agendas. Much of the discussion about resistance and opposition to racism came to the fore as research agendas evolved and engaged with radical forms of social theory in the period at the end of the twentieth century and into this century.

But this process of erasure and denial about the role of racism and colonialism in shaping present-day inequalities and divisions has its roots both in our histories and in contemporary processes. As Charles W. Mills has noted, a clear pattern of erasure and forgetting was part of the process of denial that was evident in many European countries both before and after empire. As he forcefully points out:

> The Western European nations themselves, despite being the headquarters of empire and Atlantic slavery, and the original source of modern (and perhaps premodern) racial theory, would in the post war period begin to erase their role in establishing this global racial system. In some cases (as in 'republican' France) the very legitimacy of race as a social category was denied – in fact it was deleted from the constitution in 2018 – let alone 'white supremacy' as a defensible overarching characterization. (Mills 2020: 106)

From this perspective, it is precisely this long history of forgetting and erasing the past, particularly in relation to racism, slavery and systems of racial domination that has in turn led to a relative neglect of the complex and often messy histories of resistance and rebellion against racism that helped to shape the historical experiences of many countries through the eighteenth and nineteenth centuries and beyond. Although he refers to the French context, it is also clear that this trend towards denial and erasure can be seen across many European countries with linkages to slavery and colonialism. It is a process that has involved a strange kind of silence about the long histories of racial domination that helped to shape the economic and social fabric of many European countries (Gilroy 2004; Gilroy and Oriogun-Williams 2021). With a different dynamic, there are also similar historical trends in the Americas, Africa, Australasia and beyond, where processes of enslavement and colonization have been both erased and normalized in terms of both the historical background and efforts to recover those histories for the present.

It is important to note, however, in this wider historical context, that racism as a globalized social system has often been erased not just from historical accounts but from sociological analyses of the formation and evolution of contemporary societies. As David Goldberg has noted in the context of Europe, there was an ongoing process of what he terms *racial Europeanization* that helped to shape the constitution of regional European models of racism linked to dominant state formations (Goldberg 2006). He argues that in this process it is often forgotten how central race was in the construction of modern Europe. Goldberg, and other scholars, have highlighted the many ways in which, despite differences, it is possible to grasp basic similarities in the ways that the histories of anti-Semitism, the Holocaust, slavery and the colonial experience have been a core component in the formation of nation states and the construction of national identities and myths of origin at a global level.

From a rather different angle, Barnor Hesse has developed a related strand of analysis, suggesting that racism in the European context is located both through the notion of racism as race thinking or ideological exceptionality – for example, in relation to the Nazi use of racial theories to justify their efforts to exterminate Jewish populations in Europe – and through racism based on race relations, embodied in a Western society built on practices of racism located in the European colonial experience and slavery (Hesse 2004; 2007). For Hesse, it is precisely these twin histories of race and racism that have helped to shape much of the scholarship in this field, as well as broader societal discussions about race and prejudice in the period after the Second World War.

Other scholars have sought to situate a longer history of modes of thinking about racism and antiracism that are based on contested ideas about universalist and differentialist notions of race. Michel Wieviorka, for example, develops a version of this argument, viewing the antiracist movement both historically and in the present as fractured between those who would argue for a universalist antiracism based on reason, law and equality among all citizens, and those setting off from a differential antiracism, including public space for collective identities for particular racial and ethnic groups (Wieviorka 1995). From this perspective, this kind of tension has been at the heart of debates about antiracism throughout the twentieth and the twenty-first centuries, both in terms of ideology and in the debates about what kind of policy agendas we need in order to address racial divisions and inequalities.

The broader historical background to contemporary forms of antiracism is not something that we can explore in any depth in this book. Suffice it to say, however, that the key point to be made here is that it would be wrong to assume that present-day constructions of antiracism are the only forms that it has taken. Rather, it is important to recognize that opposition to racism and the ideologies it helped to shape has been a long-standing phenomenon and it has been expressed in various forms within specific national and regional environments. This is evident in the context of the United States and Europe, but it is also an important facet of the histories of antiracism in a wider global context. There have been important and complex histories of opposition to racism and resistance through much of the period that has been shaped by European expansion and colonialism. Indeed, as will be argued in this book, we cannot fully understand the social and political forces that have shaped racialization over the past few centuries without engaging with the ways in which opposition to racism has been an integral and ongoing component of these processes.

Theorizing antiracism

Part of the challenge we face in thinking about antiracism as a concept is that it remains relatively under-theorized. There is a tendency to use the term *antiracism* somewhat descriptively. While racism as both concept and discourse has been the focus of extensive scholarly debate, antiracism remains mostly untheorized and neglected by scholarship on race and racism. Bonnett (2000), for example, argues that while racism and ethnic discrimination are under continuous historical and sociological examination, antiracism is often reduced to a social movement and narrowly defined as the inverse of racism. He also helpfully highlights the need to link the theorizing of antiracism to efforts to locate it both historically and in the contemporary environment to real-world examples and empirical research on the ways in which it has evolved and helped to shape efforts to counter racism in all its forms. Yet there remains a clear imbalance between the extensive bodies of scholarship on the formations of racism and the much more limited research that has sought to explore the evolution of antiracist modes of thought and practice.

Existing scholarship has highlighted the complex forms that antiracist mobilizations have taken in the past and in the contemporary environment. Research in both Europe and in the US has investigated the role of political and civil society mobilizations that seek to challenge everyday racism as well as its institutional forms (HoSang 2021; Lentin 2004b). These accounts have played an important role in helping to bring questions about antiracism more centrally into contemporary debates, both inside and outside the academic environment. But it is also important to explore the ways in which antiracism has been formed and influenced by both intellectual trends and everyday political and community-level struggles and protests. For starters, we need to remember that antiracism is not one thing, that there is no agreed-upon definition of what counts as antiracist. But what recent research has also shown us is that the agendas of antiracist movements and groups are heterogeneous and have been influenced by diverse ideological and political imaginaries in different historical periods (Fella and Ruzza 2013; O'Brien 2009; Twine and Blee 2001; Zamalin 2019). It is also crucial to bear in mind that, if we adopt a comparative analytical frame, there are important differences in the histories of antiracism in different national, regional and local environments. Yet there remains little research that has sought to explore the changing and shifting meanings of racism and antiracism from a comparative perspective. Some important research with a comparative focus has been done in recent years, but the impact of these bodies of work on the wider research communities remains to be seen (Lamont et al. 2016; Silva 2012). But such work has helped to highlight the value of moving towards a comparative analytical frame in exploring the processes that have shaped contemporary racisms and antiracisms.

Important points of reference in discussions of racism and antiracism are the various declarations made by the United Nations Educational, Scientific and Cultural Organization (UNESCO) in the period from 1950 to the 1970s (Hazard Jr. 2012; Montagu 1972). These statements were written by scientists and social scientists of various hues and were produced in the aftermath of the Holocaust and racial policies of the Nazi regime. Much of the language of the UNESCO statements on race sought to challenge racism and prejudice by highlighting arguments against biological ideas about race and promoting ideas about a common humanity. At the core of the various UNESCO statements was the need to use the authority of science to challenge and undermine notions about biological race differences. The 1950 and 1951 statements sought to argue that biological ideas about race should be replaced by ideas about difference in terms of ethnicity and culture. In articulating such ideas, the UNESCO statements drew on both the natural sciences and the social sciences, particularly anthropology, to argue for moving beyond race as biology to seeing race through the lens of the ways in which cultural and racial ideas were formed and shaped through social interaction and political cultures.

Although the UNESCO statements were not alone in popularizing such arguments, they did play an important role in reorienting scholarship, research and policy agendas towards ideas about race as a social relation. In doing so, they also became an important point of reference in antiracist politics and discourses as they developed in the period from the 1950s and 1960s onwards (Banton 1998; van Dijk 2021). This antiracist discourse, based as it was on a kind of cultural relativism, helped to shape emergent antiracist ideas and practices globally. It can also be argued that the core arguments that begin to be articulated in the UNESCO statements and in the growing bodies of social scientific knowledge in this period permeated political thinking as well as academic scholarship, and in many ways remain influential today. This is particularly evident in the rejection of biological ideas of race and the spread of ideologies that emphasized notions about a common humanity, in which race and ethnicity do not signal anything more than cultural differences and modes of identity formation.

There was also a kind of hope in the aftermath of the UNESCO statements and broader shifts in thinking about race that this may signal a move away from racism at a global level. In practice, although it can be argued that, within mainstream political cultures at least, a version of universalist antiracism came to be taken for granted, the shift from biological race to culture, defined in terms of separated and autonomous groups, paradoxically created the conditions for the re-articulation of what scholars such as Étienne Balibar, among others, conceptualize as forms of cultural racism, in which essentialist notions of cultures helped to re-create and legitimate new forms of racism (Balibar 2008; Balibar and Wallerstein 1991). More generally, the move towards non-biological constructions did not in itself mean that new formations of racism did not gain currency in the context of the second half of the twentieth century and the present. Rather, we saw take shape a proliferation of ideas about race that were framed around cultural and other symbolic boundaries (Hall 2017; Taguieff 2001). Although often talked about under the generic label of *new racisms* or *cultural racisms*, it is also important to note that in practice we have seen the evolution of forms of racial thinking that show elements of continuity with the past, as well as a move towards a construction of race in largely cultural terms rather than in relation to biology as such.

But it is also evident from much of the recent scholarship in this field that it is misleading to look at antiracism as shaped by a singular ideological frame. Whatever the role that the UNESCO statements on race played in influencing and shaping antiracism over the past few decades, it is also important to explore other influences. Antiracist ideas have been, and continue to be, shaped by a wide diversity of sensibilities, whether it be in the form of radical critical race theories, socialist ideas about social justice, religious values and beliefs, feminist and intersectional ideas or a whole range of other frames depending on national and localized struggles and movements. Some have their roots in specific national or local political environments, others have their origins in mobilizations by racialized minority communities, migrants and refugees. It is precisely these diverse forms of mobilization and efforts at dialogue that have enabled antiracist movements to appeal to broader sensibilities about justice and equity, as well as to specific concerns about racial inequalities and forms of exclusion.

As much of the research on various forms of antiracist activism has highlighted, many of the activists are drawn together from a variety of backgrounds, concerns, and ideological motivations. Some of those engaged in these mobilizations are young activists, others can see contemporary forms of antiracism as part of a longer history of opposition to racism and extreme right-wing politics. Some belong to majority communities, while others have everyday personal experience of racism. In short, antiracists transcend the right or left political spectrum as well as identities such as class, generation, ethnicity or professional status. Their activities are disparate and are shaped by a variety of social and political issues on the ground (Keskinen, Alemanji and Seikkula 2024; Seikkula 2022). Research on a wide spectrum of antiracist activists and organizations shows that their activities range from caring for refugees and irregular migrants, to demonstrating against a neo-fascist neighbourhood presence, developing awareness of the problem of racism in educational settings, enacting antiracist legislation, to efforts to provide better access to social and health services for vulnerable groups and individuals. Yet, despite their differing ideological and political points of departure, all of these groups link antiracism to visions of racial justice, human dignity and caring for fellow human beings caught up in positions of vulnerability and precarity.

Another underlying theme in this book will be framed by the argument that it is important to situate antiracism within both civil society and national and local state institutions in different settings. It is important, in other words, to explore cross-national similarities and differences regarding the role of specific identities – such as race, class, gender, generation and ethnicity – in creating and establishing spaces of antiracism both in everyday social relations and within institutions. While the antiracist activists and organizations often aim to challenge the responses, or non-responses, of state institutions, it is also evident from the mobilizations we have seen in recent years that a key component of their activities is organized around the need to create spaces for everyday antiracism in the context of civil society. This is evident, for example, in the activism associated with supporting refugees and irregular migrants, responding to racial violence and attacks, and in bringing diverse communities together in local settings.

From a broader analytical frame, it is also important to analyse which forms of racism are included or excluded in the diverse discourses and practices of antiracism, and how the differences and similarities create or challenge the construction of an antiracist political imaginary. Rather than assume that all antiracist mobilizations and interventions focus on the same kinds of racism, it is important to explore both similarities and differences in the way they conceive of racism and its manifestations in specific settings (Gorski 2018b; Paul 2013; St Louis 2021). This is because, in practice, there are often significant differences in the ways in which particular forms of antiracist activism define racism and construct their antiracist imaginaries, both at local and national levels.

We have seen that scholarship on antiracism is limited compared to broader scholarship on race and processes of racialization. But it is also relevant to note that in the period from the 1990s onwards we have seen important efforts to address the question of how we can theorize antiracism and its usages in contemporary societies. Scholars such as Cathie Lloyd, Floya Anthias and Alastair Bonnett broke new ground at the time with their analyses of antiracism as a body of ideas in its own right, rather than as a mirror image of racism or a response to it, as is commonly the case in much of the scholarship on antiracism (Anthias and Lloyd 2002; Bonnett 1993; 2000; Lloyd 1998). These studies focused, in particular, on the complex boundaries between antiracism, often defined in terms of radical black and ethnic politics, and forms of multiculturalism, seen as a reformist vision of cultural diversity within the realm of liberal democracy. In developing their accounts of the evolving politics of antiracism in the 1990s, they helped both to broaden our knowledge of antiracist ideas and values and to provide some much needed insight into the ideological influences that helped to shape antiracist modes of thinking both within state institutions and in the wider society.

During the 1990s and 2000s, Alastair Bonnett's work further developed this critical account of antiracism through his focus on the general development of this phenomenon as well as his research on the impact of antiracist initiatives locally and nationally in the context of education. Bonnett's work was among the first to draw attention to the distinct ideologies and ideas that helped to frame an understanding of antiracism (Bonnett 1993; 2000). In his book on *Anti-Racism*, Bonnett sought to categorize different forms of antiracism and to situate these forms within the changing political and social debates about race and immigration. In this sense, Bonnett was perhaps the first scholar to provide a rounded account of the ways in which antiracism was not in origin or in practice a singular ideological or political phenomenon. Rather, as he argued forcefully, there were in fact a diverse range of ideas and values that underpinned antiracism and helped to influence the practice both of local and national state institutions and of political and social movements. It is also worth noting that, although much of the focus in Bonnett's account was on the British context, he also engaged with key aspects of antiracist ideas and values at a more global level. In particular, he drew attention to trends and developments in the United States, Europe and South Africa.

These scholars also sought to establish the grounds for a comparative analysis of antiracism, noting in particular the emergence of diverse traditions of antiracism in the US and in Europe, and Global South and anticolonial traditions within antiracism. In developing this comparative frame, they also sought to develop an understanding of the global connections between diverse traditions of antiracist politics and discourses. Although this thread of comparative research has not developed very consistently in the period since, it highlighted a concern to move discussion beyond the confines of the Global North and to give voice to antiracisms that were developed within anticolonial, feminist and migrant political languages (Bakan and Dua 2014). This effort to shift analysis towards a more globalized perspective on antiracism is also a key thread in the work of radical black scholars who have sought to recover the often hidden histories of radical black internationalism and resistance (Kelley 1994; 2022; Makalani 2011), and to explore the national and transnational forms of these mobilizations. This growing body of scholarship has done much to highlight the important role that these forms of transnationalism played in shaping resistance in relation to both colonialism and racism.

There have also been a number of more detailed explorations of antiracism since the 2000s. This includes, in the context of the United States, efforts to provide overviews of both the history and contemporary forms of antiracism as a political discourse and ideology (Blake, Ioanide and Reed 2019; Zamalin 2019). These overviews have helpfully traced out both the longer-term and more recent forms of antiracist mobilization at all levels of society, including political, social and cultural interventions to tackle specific types of discrimination and exclusion. These have been complemented by detailed accounts of antiracist movements that took place in the second half of the twentieth century, as well as more recent times. We shall turn to some of these mobilizations and their impact in chapters 2 and 3.

We have seen similar trends in scholarly research in other contexts. In the context of Europe, for example, scholars such as Alana Lentin (Lentin 2000; 2004a; 2004b) locate the study of antiracism in the changing political environment of the past few decades, characterized by the escalation of Islamophobia, the creation of hostile environments for migrants and refugees, and the growth of new forms of racist social movements that target racialized minorities and other excluded groups. From this perspective, antiracism is seen as being shaped by these broader developments, as well as helping to shape them in turn. This strand of research has been particularly influential in the past two decades as researchers have focused attention on antiracist mobilizations concerned with migrant rights and Islamophobia (Harris 2021). In the UK as well as the broader European environment, much of the discussion of antiracism over the past decade has taken on a somewhat different tone from the conversations that have come to the fore in the US.

Such studies have helped to develop our understandings of antiracism and its workings in practice. But there are still notable gaps and absences in these emerging bodies of research, and there still seems to be a relative lack of theorization of the role of social relations, class, gender, ethnicity, generation, identities and specific communities in the making of antiracism. It is also the case that much of the research on antiracism has been focused on the work of white antiracist organizations and activists, with the voices of racialized minorities and migrants remaining relatively marginal in much of the research in this field. This has begun to change in recent years, with more research focusing on the role of racialized minorities in antiracist movements and mobilizations, as well as in other forms of political and community-based activities.

Antiracism in perspective

A key argument that will be advanced in this book is that we cannot really make sense of antiracism, both as a set of ideas and values and as policy interventions, without a broader understanding of the historical and contemporary forms of racism and efforts to tackle it. It is important, in other words, to situate an analysis of antiracism within a broader analytical frame against the background of the formation of racism in different historical environments, as well as its impact on social and political relations in the present. It is important to see the histories of racism and antiracism as interlinked, not just in terms of ideas but also at the political and institutional level. Given our focus in this book on antiracism, we shall not revisit in detail the rich body of scholarship that has sought to provide a critical analytical frame for the analysis of contemporary expressions of racism at both social and political levels (Goldberg 2009; Lentin 2020; Solomos 2023; Virdee 2014). But it is important to note that our starting point in this book is premised on a wider body of research that has explored the changing forms of racism, and indeed antiracism, over the past century and more. These bodies of scholarship have explored both the efforts to tackle racism in practice and at the level of policy, and the relative failure in terms of the overall objective of achieving equality and racial justice at all levels of the social world around us.

As we have noted above, there are ongoing debates about the social and political role of racialized inequalities and divisions and the measures needed to tackle them. This has been a feature of public policy debate ever since the important transformations that were made in the 1960s and 1970s, and these conversations continue into the present day. But it is also the case that in the decades that followed we saw ongoing discussions about how best to tackle key sites of racialized inequality in a wide range of societies.

In the context of the US, an important point of reference in the aftermath of the Civil Rights Movement has been the Report of the Kerner Commission from 1968, as well as a number of other influential reports over the past few decades (Fogelson, Black and Lipsky 1969; Kerner Commission 2016; Reed Jr. 2017). Although the Kerner Report was published in the aftermath of the riots of the 1960s and at the high point of the Civil Rights Movement, it has remained a key text for those who are concerned with the ongoing struggles to tackle the persistence of racialized social and economic inequalities. It is also often seen as providing a symbolic statement of the relative failure to address the longer-term consequences of racial divisions and tensions around race in American society.

In Britain, the publication of the classic *Colour & Citizenship* signalled the importance of both governmental and civil society initiatives to tackle the root causes of racialized inequalities and divisions (Rose 1968; 1969). This was, in hindsight, the first of a number of benchmark reports that sought to provide overviews of the changing forms of racial inequalities and division in British society. Examples of these reports include the Scarman Report on the riots of 1980–1, the Macpherson Report on the death of Stephen Lawrence, the Parekh Report on the future of multi-ethnic Britain, and the more recent Sewell Report on racial and ethnic disparities (Commission on Race and Ethnic Disparities 2021; Macpherson 1999; Parekh 2000; Scarman 1981). An underlying concern in all of these reports, although they are framed within different ideological standpoints, is how to progress towards a policy agenda that addresses questions about racial and ethnic divisions in key social and political arenas in the wider society.

But it is also important to note that antiracism is not a preoccupation unique to American or British society, since the question of how we can move beyond racism is an ongoing point of discussion and debate across a wide range of societies in the contemporary environment. There is a wealth of research, both theoretical and empirical, that is focused on the workings of racisms from both a historical angle and in the present. Yet, there remains relatively little discussion about the possibilities for moving beyond racism and the ways that this may be achieved. In the context of the United States, the public debates about Black Lives Matter and critical race theory have brought questions about the continuing significance of racial inequalities and the role of policies that can tackle their root causes to the fore in both local and national political debates. At the same time, mobilizations around such issues as police violence and the criminal justice system have helped to emphasize the contested nature of race and racial divisions in the contemporary conjuncture. It should be noted that the outbreak of the Covid-19 pandemic brought to the fore the question of forms of racialized inequalities in terms of health.

This book seeks to make a critical intervention in these ongoing debates about the continuing significance of racialized divisions and the role of the institutional processes and ideologies that have helped to maintain them in contemporary societies. At the level of public policies, various policy agendas over in recent years have promised to tackle racial discrimination and inequalities, both in specific areas such as employment, housing and health and in other social arenas. At the same time there has been an ongoing debate about policies aimed at promoting a vision of a multicultural and multiethnic sense of national identity that is inclusive of racialized minorities.

Yet there is also at the same time a wealth of empirical evidence and research that has provided support for the argument that, whatever the impact of these policies and initiatives, there remain entrenched and institutionalized forms of racial inequalities that run through society and intersect with class, gender and ethnic divisions. The publication in 2021 of the report of the Commission on Race and Ethnic Disparities in the United Kingdom, for example, and the public furore surrounding it have helped to highlight the contested nature of these questions in the contemporary political environment (Commission on Race and Ethnic Disparities 2021). The report also helped to develop a wider conversation about the kinds of policies that are needed in the contemporary environment.

Much of the scholarship and research over the past few decades has focused on how racism and racialization work through and intersect with other categories such as gender, class, ethnicity, religion and nation. This has helped to provide an understanding of the workings of processes of racialization and ethnicization and the way they work in contemporary societies. As a result of this growing body of scholarship, we have a better understanding of the institutional and everyday processes that help to produce and reproduce racisms as a social phenomenon. As a result of the work of scholars such as Stuart Hall, David Goldberg and Paul Gilroy, we are also more informed about how racisms evolve and are transformed across time and place, appearing often in multiple forms (Gilroy 2004; Goldberg and Giroux 2014; Hall 2017).

Yet it remains the case that we do not have a clear and focused understanding of the role of antiracist politics and mobilizations in contemporary societies or in the future. Indeed, despite the noticeable expansion of scholarship and research in this broad field over the first three decades of the twenty-first century, there is clear need for more discussion of the development of antiracist politics and imaginaries that seek to address the issue of whether we can move beyond racism. This is partly the result of the ways in which much critical scholarship in this field remains embedded in political languages about moving beyond capitalism rather than acting to reform and change actually existing societies, resulting in little discussion about the possibilities and limits of antiracism. While it can be argued that it is important to remain focused on the continuing role of racism and racial inequalities, it will be argued in this book that this should not be at the cost of a critical understanding of the evolution of antiracism both at the level of policy and in the context of civil society.

A key thread in this book is that we need to re-focus empirical research and scholarly agendas not only to address the ways in which racisms and antiracisms are made and re-made but to look more closely at how we can begin conversations about how to move beyond racism. If we want to end racism and racial disparities, we need to understand processes of racialization, but we also need to know more about the proposed solution – namely, antiracism. As a number of critical race scholars have shown, there is little evidence that we are seeing a transition to a post-racial future where racialized inequalities and divisions will diminish in importance in all spheres of society (Goldberg 2015; 2021; Meghji and Niang 2022; Sayyid 2017). At the same time, however, I shall argue that it is important to avoid the tendency to see racism as omnipresent, since this tends to devalue the achievements of antiracist policies and struggles for change and reform over the past few decades.

But there is nevertheless a need to develop a somewhat more nuanced account that brings questions about antiracism and its futures more centrally into research and policy agendas. Some of the key questions that will be addressed in the book are: How has antiracism been understood and defined? What does antiracism mean in different local, national, transnational contexts? What role do racialized groups, ethnic minorities and migrants play in shaping antiracism in theory and practice? How do states and civil society define and practise antiracism? What is the role of alliances across race, class and gender in shaping possible futures beyond racism? How do political institutions and civil society institutions define and practise antiracism? These are all complex questions in their own right but we shall aim to explore them together in this book in order to address the overarching question that frames its theoretical and empirical concerns – namely, how we move beyond racism and develop more just and equal societies.

As has been argued thus far, the making of contemporary forms of antiracism has taken place in a political and social context that provided room for the expression of ideas and values that challenged racism in all its forms, from the institutional to the personal. A good example of the importance of placing antiracism in this broader context can be found in the United States through much of the twentieth century as well as in the present. It is also clear, however, that other trajectories of antiracism can be traced outside of the Global North. There were important and impactful mobilizations of antiracist ideas and movements in South Africa through much of the twentieth century, including the long period of institutionalized segregation by the apartheid regime. It is also important to note the complex unfolding of mobilizations about race and racism in the context of Brazil, particularly at the end of the twentieth century and the beginning of this century (Hanchard 1994; van Dijk 2020).

The changing politics of antiracism

The changing politics around antiracism in the contemporary environment can be traced to trends and developments that came to the fore at the end of the twentieth century and the beginning of the twenty-first. It is in this period that we saw increasing public controversy about antiracism and the policy agendas associated with it. This can be seen partly in the ways that over the past decade we have seen a growth both of mobilizations under the banner of antiracism as well as of growing opposition to antiracist initiatives by new right and neo-conservative activists.

Given this broader political environment, it is not surprising that commentators from the right of the political spectrum have sought to argue that policies framed around antiracist and multicultural values have failed and become in themselves a source of division and discord. Politicians from the right have increasingly talked of the failures of antiracist policies and interventions and dismissed them as part of the problem rather than a solution. The highly charged debates about race and immigration in the United States, both during and after the Trump presidency from 2016 to 2020, are an example of the increasingly politicized debates in this field over the past two decades. In the divisive political atmosphere that was evident during this period, and in many ways continues today, mobilizations around issues such as racial inequality and exclusion, or the protection of refugees and migrants, became the site of intense debate about the future not just of race relations but of American society more generally (Smith and King 2024). Although the tone of these debates has changed somewhat under the Biden administration from 2020 onwards, it is also clear that questions about race remain a seriously divisive issue in American society, with deeply entrenched positions and little or no dialogue between them. Given the absence of much dialogue across the massive divide around race that has become evident over the past decade and more, we have seen a noticeable entrenchment of political positions that seems to be helping to shape broader tensions across American society.

Another example of this can be found in the interventions of right-wing ethnic-minority Conservative politicians in the UK, such as Suella Braverman and Kemi Badenoch, over the past few years, on questions about racial inequalities and disparities (Badenoch 2021; Braverman 2023a; 2023b). The tone of these interventions involves both accepting the realities of what they choose to term 'racial disparities' rather than racism, while at the same time denying that they can be connected to the legacies or the contemporary forms of structural racism as such. Badenoch, for example, responded to the report of the Commission on Race and Ethnic Disparities (Commission on Race and Ethnic Disparities 2021) by arguing that 'While disparities between ethnic groups exist across numerous areas, many factors other than racism are often the root cause. Among these are geography, deprivation, and family structure. For example, a Black Caribbean child is ten times more likely than an Indian child to grow up in a lone parent household' (Badenoch 2021).

From this perspective, the core question we face today is not how to tackle racism and its impact on racialized minorities, but facets of the family and cultural deficiencies to be found in particular communities. While such accounts also accept the realities of growing forms of racial and ethnic diversity in British society (Sunak and Rajeswaran 2014), they are also often focused on the need to exclude refugees and irregular migrants through harsh measures to deter them from coming to the UK. Indeed, a defining feature of the current situation in British society is that there seems to be a kind of consensus across the political divides that irregular migrants and refugees are not welcome, even as these same political ideologies argue that we have moved beyond racism and that we should celebrate racial, religious and cultural diversities in our society. It is a mixture of these concerns and preoccupations that led to this book being framed in the way it is, as both an exploration of the various meanings that have been attached to the idea of antiracism and a critical intervention about the possibilities for radical antiracisms to impact on the societies in which we live in the present. It is for this reason that this book is focused on global developments, although I shall use illustrative examples from the UK, Europe, North America, Latin America, South Africa and beyond in order to provide a flavour of the ongoing conversations and controversies around antiracism. It is also an effort to argue that we need ongoing research and scholarly agendas that address the question of what kinds of antiracist policy interventions we need to address the deep-seated racialized inequalities in contemporary societies.

The key objective of this book is to intervene in the ongoing conversations, both academic and policy-related, about antiracism, and to suggest ways forward. Given the wide-ranging discussions over the past decade and more, about such issues as racial inequality, Black Lives Matter and the growth of racist movements and ideologies, it is important to address the question of antiracism more fully than has been the case in much of the scholarship on racial and ethnic questions over the first few decades of the twenty-first century.

It is also important, as we shall argue throughout this book, to tackle head on the issue of what we can do in practice, to imagine what the *end of racism* may look like in different societies, in the institutions of the public and private sectors and in the context of civil society. These are not in themselves new questions as such, since antiracism has been part of political and policy debates about race and racial inequality both historically and over the past half-century or so.

Indeed, as historical research has shown, antiracist imaginaries were an integral component of both scholarly and policy debates. During the past few decades, we have seen ongoing conversations about the persistence of racism and racialized inequalities in a wide range of societies. In the aftermath of the Civil Rights Movement in the US and similar mobilizations in other countries, there was a kind of optimism through the 1970s and 1980s that the legacies and structures of racism were being tackled through political, legal and policy interventions. In the decades since, however, there has been increasing recognition that institutionalized forms of racism at all levels of society, including the public and private sectors, remain deeply entrenched and persist despite the policy agendas that have sought to address them in a wide range of arenas in contemporary societies. In particular, through the first decades of the twenty-first century, there has been an increasing focus on questions about what can be done to tackle these persistent racialized inequalities at all levels of society. This focus has in turn been highlighted by mobilizations that have been framed around the need to develop new political and policy agendas for tackling racism in the present and the reasons that it persists and shapes social and political relations in the world around us.

Such mobilizations have often been framed by a commitment to tackle racism and promote strategies for achieving equality of opportunity. Often focused round policy arenas in education, employment and housing, the main concern has been to achieve change through both legal and educational interventions aimed at addressing evident disparities and inequalities. Governments of various political hues have embraced ideas about addressing racial inequalities and disadvantage, the promotion of multiculturalism and broader ideologies about moving beyond race and promoting the interests of diverse groups in society. In doing so, they have often framed their policies around political commitments to tackle inequalities in particular areas of society, as well as more generalized agendas to provide equal opportunities for all citizens regardless of race, gender, class, sexuality and other social and cultural characteristics.

Across a range of societies in Europe, North America, Latin America, Southern Africa and Asia, we have seen policy initiatives premised on values that oppose racism and seek to provide a policy frame for addressing racialized inequalities. Although some of these commitments can be seen as largely exercises in symbolic politics, at another level they have also reflected commitments to tackle entrenched inequalities that are seen as potentially ideas about equality and equal opportunity. In the United States, for example, we have seen efforts over the past three decades by both the Obama and the Biden administrations to highlight their commitment to build on the advances in racial equality made in the 1960s and 1970s, in order to tackle the persistence of racialized inequalities and to address ongoing issues, such as deadly police violence that impacts African Americans and other racialized minorities. There has been much debate about the success of these interventions in practice, but at a basic level both administrations sought to highlight their commitment to tackle the legacies of past racial divisions and to address current issues, including inequalities in relation to criminal justice, health, education, wealth and related social issues.

In the context of British society, the first three decades of the twenty-first century have seen interventions, both by the Labour governments of the early 2000s and by the Conservative-led administrations since 2010, that have been framed around the need to tackle such issues as *social cohesion, racial inequalities* and *ethnic disparities* (Back, Keith, Shukra and Solomos 2023: 25; Bloch, Neal and Solomos 2013). These conversations have become increasingly politicized and divisive since they are an integral part of broader debates about the politics of race, immigration and multiculturalism.

But they have signalled, albeit from very different ideological standpoints, a broad commitment to address social inequalities shaped by race and ethnic divisions in areas such as education, health and employment.

An important theme in these conversations has been the question of what kind of policies and practices can be developed in order to tackle the root causes of racialized divisions in the world around us. A recurrent point of reference in these conversations has been focused on the question of antiracism, both as a set of ideas and values and as policy agendas and interventions (Kundnani 2023; Zamalin 2019). For some, particularly on the left, antiracism has taken on the meaning of a radical policy agenda that is premised on how to eradicate the institutionalized forms of racism that have become entrenched at all levels of our society, whether at the social, economic or political levels. From this perspective, antiracism is seen as presenting a radical alternative to limited multicultural, and ultimately ineffective post-racial, policy agendas (Bhattacharyya, Virdee and Winter 2020; Hage 2015). For others, particularly on the right, antiracism has become a symbol of a politics that is focused on the interests of racialized minorities, as opposed to those of the white majorities (Ehsan 2023; Goodhart 2017; 2019; Kaufmann 2018). For some of these commentators, antiracism has become part of the problem, at least in the sense that liberal elites have adopted it as part of their political agenda and promoted it against the interests of the white majority and the nation.

We have engaged in previous research with the question of how antiracist mobilizations and forms of resistance to racism can change ideologies about race and the structures of racialized inequalities, particularly in empirical studies about the politics of race at local and national levels, racism and football cultures, and race and social policy. Indeed, through much of this research, we have also had to address the question of what kind of policies and political interventions we need in order to tackle both institutional and everyday forms of racism in contemporary societies. In thinking about these issues, we have been forced to think more critically about what kind of antiracist initiatives we need in the context of contemporary controversies about the persistence of racialized inequalities and divisions. This has in turn led us to explore both the origins of antiracism, the development of political movements against racism and the evolving meanings of antiracist thinking in the present environment.

At the same time, I have also engaged in teaching various generations of students about both the history and contemporary forms of racism and antiracism, in Britain, the United States and other geopolitical contexts. In much of this teaching, discussion and conversations have inevitably come back in one way or another to the question of what impact policies framed around ideas about multiculturalism and antiracism can have in tackling the structures of racism that shape the world around us. In the course of this teaching, we have engaged in conversations about the possibilities for developing policy agendas that can tackle the persistence of racism as a set of ideas and values, as well as the structures of racialized inequalities that have been produced both historically and in the present.

Given these experiences, I have been thinking for some time that there is a need for a book that addressed antiracism directly, both conceptually and in terms of practice. This book is the outcome of this feeling that we need to devote more attention to the analysis of antiracism if we are going to be able to make sense of the social and political debates about race and racism in the world around us. In this sense, it has been shaped by my experience as a researcher, teacher and scholar. But it has also been informed by trends and developments in the wider social and political environment where we have seen only limited discussion about antiracism as a set of ideas and values, and even less analysis of what kinds of antiracist practices may help to bring about change in the world around us. Indeed, over the past few decades, I have seen little informed discussion of antiracism, even as scholarly research on racial and ethnic relations has expanded and become institutionalized. It is with an eye on this relative absence of discussion about antiracism that I decided to write this short book, with the hope that it will contribute to ongoing discussions about how best to tackle the root causes of racism and racialized inequalities in contemporary societies.

Thinking beyond antiracism

Another issue that will be addressed in this book is the question of how we can begin to think beyond antiracism. In developing this strand of analysis, we shall engage with the growing bodies of scholarship about how we can engage with the practicalities of moving beyond both racism and antiracism through the creation of societies shaped by racial justice and equity. Part of the challenge that arises when thinking about both the immediate and longer-term objectives of antiracism is that the objective of antiracist mobilizations is often linked to the broad ideas of finding ways to eliminate racism, or at least to reduce its impact on the social and class relations that shape contemporary societies.

In a recent intervention, Paul Gilroy has captured some of the key tensions that are part of the ongoing conversations about antiracism, whether in specific nation states or in a more globalized sense. Gilroy's starting point is to warn against the dangers of using concepts such as antiracism to discuss the complex range of challenges we face in the contemporary social and political environment regarding how we deal with differences shaped by multiple migrations and processes of racialization. In a critical exploration of the situation facing migrants and refugees attempting to cross the Mediterranean for the shores of Europe, Gilroy argues that there is a need for a fundamental rethinking of the language of antiracism in the present, particularly in a context where ideas about care and humanity have challenged us to think about the limits of what he calls *planetary humanism*. He makes the point that: 'What should no longer be called antiracism must re-make itself in a more daring mode capable of displaying and summoning the world we need' (Gilroy 2022: 120).

In rejecting the very language of antiracism, Gilroy is suggesting that there is a need to develop new ways of talking about the possibilities of caring and valuing the humanity of others. He is also pointing to the need to ask questions about what antiracism actually means in this ever changing environment, and what kinds of futures are likely to be constructed through antiracist policies and interventions.

Given the complex processes that Gilroy and others have drawn attention to, it is important to remain aware that the language used in antiracist discourses may make it difficult to begin the process of thinking beyond antiracism. This is partly because, as we have argued, we need to be open to the reality that antiracism is not, and has never been, a monolithic phenomenon. By focusing this book on antiracism, we aim to capture not only how racism is defined and made into an idea, object and practice to struggle against, but also how antiracism can be understood as a productive vision shaping ideas about what our societies could aim to achieve in terms of racial justice, both today and in the future.

In this context, we should also remember that antiracism is difficult to address without an understanding of the workings of racism both in historical terms and in the present. Following Stuart Hall (Hall 1980; 2017; Hall, Gilroy and Gilmore 2021), we read the concept of racism in its plural form, racisms, emphasizing how racism as a social phenomenon is transformed across time and place, appearing as it does in multiple forms. The changing forms of racism have also been constructed through the concepts of racialization and ethnicization to capture the processes through which notions of race and ethnicity are used to construct groups and to delimit differences. The spread of identity politics in a context of new processes of racialization also raises questions about how individuals interpret belonging and group membership in the context of the increasingly diverse societies that have emerged in the contemporary period.

It is also important to note that much of the scholarship on race and racism over the past few decades has explored the development of new forms of racism. In particular there has been increased focus on the development of forms of cultural racism, namely the idea that individuals are bearers of an innate, static culture associated with their ethnic, religious or racial identities (Hall 2017; Solomos 2023). Part of the underlying assumption of these new forms of racism is that these cultures determine identities and behaviour. There has also been renewed interest in the role of everyday forms of racism, where minorities are avoided, discriminated against, or excluded based on their assumed difference. Another important focus is the link between racism and nationalism, and how transnational travel, colonial relations and present-day migrations challenge the idea of entrenched national communities and broadly shared ideas of belonging. Understandings of racism, however, remain poorly conceptualized within studies of antiracist social movements, and the extant literature has not adequately addressed how definitions of racism are subject to contestation tied to issues of historicity and legitimacy. There has been little focus on how internal and external struggles in antiracist movements continually seek to renegotiate conceptualizations of racism in the mobilization process, and the way in which the framing of racism intertwines with broader social imaginaries.

As we explore these issues in this book, we shall argue that it is important to pay close attention to the range of meanings that are attached to the notion of antiracism in specific political and institutional contexts. While, for some commentators, antiracism is seen as the negation of racism, for others it has other meanings, including the celebration of ethnic and cultural differences, the annulment of race and ethnicity as a hierarchical principle of social organization, and at a broader level the implementation of policies aimed at promoting racial justice and equity. The proliferation of meanings attached to antiracism highlights both its contested nature and the unfinished debates about the best way to address the social and political consequences of racism in today's global environment. But as we shall see it is precisely this contested nature of antiracism that can allow us to develop a fuller understanding of the challenges that we face in tackling both structural and individual expressions of racism.

Before moving on to the discussion of the core issues that frame this book, I shall now briefly outline the key themes that each of the following chapters seeks to cover.

Key themes and chapter outline

Thus far, I have outlined the core questions and themes that provide the overarching frame for the book as a whole. In particular, I have argued that there is a need for conversations both about the complex histories of antiracism and about what kinds of antiracism have emerged and taken shape in the present. In developing this narrative, I have touched on the key themes that we shall return to in the chapters that follow as we explore both the historical background to antiracist movements and mobilizations and the changing meanings and sensibilities attached to antiracism. We have also seen that we need to focus on developing a wider historical, empirical and theoretical research agenda about antiracism that can help us to move on from current preoccupations and progress towards developing greater clarity about what a society that has moved beyond racism may look like in practice. Before going further, however, it is important to briefly outline the structure of the book as a whole in order to guide readers.

Chapter 2 moves on from the issues discussed thus far to outline the changing forms of antiracism in the present. It begins by discussing the relationship between racism and antiracism, and it then provides a grounded account of the forms of antiracism that have come to the fore in contemporary societies, the relationship between these expressions of antiracism, and the changing political debates that have emerged in the current conjuncture about questions around race and racism. It is here that we shall seek to develop a critical discussion of what antiracism has been taken to mean and the evolution of political debates about the changing boundaries of antiracism.

From this discussion, we then move on in *chapter 3* to a critical analysis of efforts to put antiracist strategies and policies into practice, whether at the level of movements and ideas or through policy interventions aimed at state institutions or other sectors of society. Under the rubric of this chapter, we shall also explore what kinds of policies have been developed to tackle the institutionalized racial inequalities that have remained a part of our societies even after decades of efforts to tackle them in practice. In analysing these evolving policy and political agendas, we shall address efforts to challenge both institutional and everyday forms of racism. A recurrent question at the heart of this chapter is the issue of what is meant by the notion of putting antiracism into practice. We shall also explore the limits and contradictions that are evident in the efforts to develop antiracist policies and ways through which they can be fruitfully addressed.

Chapter 4 tackles head on a question at the heart of this book – namely, the issue of what has been achieved after all the antiracist mobilizations and policy interventions that we have seen over the past few decades. We shall argue that, while

there is little evidence that we have moved towards the elimination of racism, there are important ways in which antiracism
has impacted on social and political institutions, albeit often in
an uneven manner. In developing this account, we shall also
address the question of how to broaden antiracist policy and
political agendas, including the impact of intersectional perspectives and efforts to engage the corporate and professional
sectors. In exploring these critiques, we shall also address the
emergence of what is sometimes called anti-antiracism, as
reflected in efforts from the political right to deny the relevance
of antiracist ideas and values in contemporary societies. What
such criticisms seek to do, above all, is to refocus attention not
on racism as such but on what they see as the dangers of antiracism as an ideology. We shall argue that such anti-antiracist
perspectives are often tied into denials of the importance of
racism in the present and a tendency to see the future through
a post-racial lens. In this context, debates about antiracism
have become entangled with broader controversies about such
issues as racial inequalities, immigration and national identity.
In the present climate, it is important to address such denials
head on and provide an evidence base for the need for radical
measures to tackle racism.

Chapter 5 concludes the book by bringing together the core
arguments it outlines as well as looking forwards to what kinds
of antiracism we shall need to develop to tackle pressing questions about both the present and the future of our societies. In
developing this account, the chapter provides a twin-pronged
exploration of the politics of antiracism in the current conjuncture as well as looking at the question of what kind of
policy and political agendas we need to develop for the future.
It concludes by arguing that a re-imagining of antiracism needs
to bring to the fore conversations about how we can best move
beyond racialized divisions and inequalities in specific societies
as well as in the wider global environment. In looking forwards,
we shall also engage with the need for a radical antiracism to

address the need to change the world around us rather than imagine some kind of post-capitalist or post-racial future that is not grounded in the everyday realities of the present. In discussing the contested nature of antiracism, we shall address both radical critiques of antiracism and right-wing efforts to question the need for any antiracist policies and interventions.

2

Antiracisms in the Present

Thus far, we have concentrated on outlining the background and historical context of antiracism and its relation to ongoing research and political debates about racism. In addition, we have also touched on the evolution of different theoretical frames that have sought to make sense of what the idea of antiracism has meant and what it could mean in the future. By exploring these themes, a key argument that we have sought to highlight is the need to move away from a monolithic view of antiracism and to see it as a phenomenon that is expressed in various forms within specific countries, at the national and local scale, and on a global scale. In doing so, it was argued that there is a need to locate the evolution of the various forms of antiracism within the wider historical context of racism in all its forms and the growth of oppositional ideologies that have sought to challenge the persistence of racial inequalities and racism both at the institutional level and in the political ideologies in contemporary societies.

The connections between the related histories of racism and antiracism have become even more evident over the past few decades in the context of ongoing debates about what, if anything, can be done to tackle persistent concerns about racialized inequalities in key social arenas, including employment, education, housing, health and criminal justice. Indeed, through much of the period since the beginning of the twenty-first century, a recurrent area of public debate has been the question of how we can best tackle the structural and institutional forms of racialized division and exclusion. This has, perhaps, been most evident in societies such as the US, particularly around key policy areas linked to criminal justice, policing, employment and education (Andersen 2021; Desmond and Emirbayer 2015; Golash-Boza 2016). But there have also been important debates around related issues across Europe, Brazil, Latin America, and other parts of the globe (Bonnett 2022; Solomos 2020). It is for this reason that we have emphasized the need to see antiracism through a comparative lens, since it is not a phenomenon that can be understood merely through its national forms, given the often global perspectives that have helped to shape antiracist ideologies and values through much of the twentieth century and into the present. Part of the need for such a comparative frame is highlighted by the ways in which research and policy debates about the general phenomenon of antiracism often take place in isolation, with researchers rarely engaging even in open conversations about what they can learn from each other.

This chapter moves on to delve more deeply into the evolving expressions of antiracism in the contemporary social and political environment. In order to lay the foundations for the rest of this analysis, we shall begin by discussing the relationship between contemporary forms of racism and evolving expressions of antiracism. We then critically engage with efforts to define the various forms that antiracist mobilizations and practices have taken over the past few decades. This allows us to then discuss the changing politics of antiracism, particularly in the context of the ongoing conversations about how we can move forwards in developing policies and interventions that can help us to imagine and shape alternative futures beyond racism. From these starting points, we shall then move on to tackle the relationship between the wide range of anti-racist mobilizations and forms of resistance to racism that have emerged on a global scale in recent times.

Racisms and antiracisms

Before going on any further, it is important to briefly discuss a key point that we have touched upon already – namely, the argument that racisms and antiracisms are inextricably linked, in terms of both histories and their contemporary expressions. A key point to bear in mind in any analysis of antiracism is that it can only be understood on the basis of locating it against the background of its opposite – namely, racism. Both historically and in the present, questions about racism and antiracism have become inevitably interlinked through ongoing conversations in the political sphere and through the ways in which we can make sense of them through their interactions, both structurally and at the level of ideas and movements. This argument has formed part of scholarly analysis among both historians and sociologists who have explored the complex histories of racism both globally and in specific national contexts (Bonnett 2022; Fredrickson 1997; 2002). The interconnections between racisms and antiracisms have become evident both at the institutional level and in everyday debates about how to deal with questions such as policing, health inequalities and access to education.

This is why it is imperative to move away from a conception that antiracism is a singular phenomenon. This means recognizing that there are in practice a broad range of ideological and political frames that have helped to shape antiracism in the world around us, both historically and in the present. These include political ideologies shaped by ideas about a common humanity, by class-based social movements, religious and cultural values, black liberation, and resistance and opposition to racist movements and organizations.

From a historical perspective, it is also important to remember that there have been other influences that were shaped by the intertwined histories of slavery, colonialism and imperialism. The evolution of opposition to slavery and colonialism found expression in ideologies that sought to undermine both the structures and ideologies that sustained them. Through the tumultuous periods encompassed by the eighteenth, nineteenth and twentieth centuries, we saw the growth of oppositional forces that articulated anti-colonialism, anti-imperialism and ideas against slavery. The growth of anti-colonial movements during the first half of the twentieth century reflected this diversity of ideas, particularly since such movements were shaped both by opposition to ideas of European supremacy and by various nationalist and ethnic ideologies at the same time. In the more contemporary period too, opposition to racist movements and ideologies was often influenced by ideas of opposition to neo-Nazi and neo-fascist ideologies of race. Such mobilizations against extreme right-wing movements helped to sustain the idea that opposition to racism should be based on ideas about a common humanity, caring for racialized or excluded others, and developing critical understandings of the role of racism and xenophobia in society.

It is also necessary to avoid the temptation to see racism as a uniform and unchanging set of ideas and values, since in practice it has been evident over the past few centuries that it is best to see racism as constantly evolving and taking on new ideological meanings. Historians such as George Mosse have famously defined racism as a kind of scavenger ideology that takes on ideas from different political movements, traditions and philosophies (Mosse 1985). It is for this reason that a growing number of scholars talk of *racisms* rather than *racism*. Indeed, over the past few decades, a large and growing body of scholarship has helpfully sought to explore the changing forms of racism in contemporary societies. In particular, we have seen ongoing debates and controversies about what can broadly be defined as *new racisms* or *cultural racisms* as they are expressed in everyday social and political discourses. Although many of the racisms that are articulated under the banner of new racism are not in themselves that new, it is also clear that in the period since the second half of the twentieth century, racism has increasingly been expressed through ideas about cultural differences and separations between racial and ethnic groups.

In this broader historical context as well as in the present, it is important to take on board the idea that, in practice, racism is not a singular and unchanging phenomenon, since in practice we see a range of racisms at work in different societies. There has been a recurring theoretical debate going back to the 1970s and 1980s that has focused on the question of whether we have seen the articulation of new racisms framed much more around notions of culture and difference and less on the traditional tropes that helped to frame classical racist ideologies, from the nineteenth through the twentieth centuries (Ansell 1997; Balibar and Wallerstein 1991; Barker 1981). This debate has taken on various forms in the decades since, particularly in relation to the changing political and civil society transformations that we have seen in the United States, Europe and more globally, in the ways that racism is being expressed and articulated, both politically and through social movements. Key transformations in the ways that racism is being expressed occurred in the last few decades of the twentieth century and continue into the present. More recently, we have seen the articulation of new modes of racist thinking that have attempted to utilize forms of ethnonationalism and cultural separatism in order to justify ideas premised on differentialist discourses that seek to distance themselves from the language of racial superiority and white superiority.

Alongside these debates about new racisms, we have seen a second conversation about whether in the contemporary social and political environment we are seeing the emergence of a *post-racial* present and future in various societies (Goldberg 2015). In the United States, this discussion about the *post-racial* became prominent both during, and in the immediate aftermath of, the election of Barack Obama in 2008 as the first black president, and has continued in various forms in the period since as we have seen the emergence and evolution of a new politics around race and racism (Crenshaw 2019a; Pettigrew 2009; Smith and King 2009). In the context of European societies, there has also been an ongoing conversation about whether we are seeing the development of a *post-racial conjuncture* as we see the development of new forms of multiculturalism, greater cultural and religious diversity, and new political discourses about race. Although somewhat different in tone and in context from the debates going on in American society, this conversation has highlighted issues that remain at the heart of contemporary social and political debates in present-day Europe. The contested nature of immigration and national identity is perhaps the issue at the heart of conversations in the European context. The role of race in these ongoing debates has been somewhat different from the longer history of such conversations in the United States, though it is also evident, over the past two decades or so, that despite some silences on race, there are also clear connections between the preoccupations evident in both settings.

These are somewhat contrasting strands of debate, and they are suggestive of very different research and political agendas. Yet in a sense they are connected by a common concern to understand what is changing and what remains the same in the expression of contemporary forms of racism. Both strands of analysis have taken shape in the context of the transformations we have seen around questions of racial and ethnic relations in the period since the early 2000s, and they are therefore very much live issues. More importantly, they highlight the significance of understanding the making of race in the present, and the necessity to develop conceptual tools that will allow us to make sense of the challenges that we face today, as well as the issues that may lie beyond the horizon that will need to be included in these conversations soon.

The scholarship on new forms of racism shows how contemporary manifestations of race are coded in a language which aims to circumvent accusations of racism. In the case of new racisms, it is often the case that race is coded as culture. However, the central feature of these processes is that the qualities of social groups are fixed, made natural, confined within a pseudo-biologically defined culturalism. What is clear from these writings is that a range of discourses on social differentiation may have a metonymic relationship to racism. The semantics of race are produced by a complex set of interdiscursive processes where the language of culture and nation invokes a hidden racial narrative. The defining feature of this process is the way in which it naturalizes social formations in terms of a racial-cultural logic of identity and belonging. It is this process of naturalization that also characterizes the discourses of contemporary racist movements, although often combined with the remnants and traces of ideas about race expressed in pseudo-scientific and biological language at the same time.

Forms of antiracism

It is against this broader environment that we need to see the evolution and development of various forms of antiracism. During the second half of the twentieth century, we saw the emergence and evolution of a wide range of antiracist movements and political movements and ideas. These movements were formed and evolved in a broader political environment where they saw themselves as responding to and countering the activities of both extreme right-wing and overtly racist movements (Anthias and Lloyd 2002; Lloyd 1998). This reflected the increasingly politicized and fractious nature of political and policy debates about race, immigration and multiculturalism. But it is also important to note that, as antiracist mobilizations took shape, they were not characterized by one set of ideas and values and took inspiration from a wide range of sources. Although often seen as part of left-wing social movements that came to the fore during this same period, this is somewhat misleading. In reality, antiracist movements were shaped by a diverse range of concerns – local, national and global. They were inspired both by developments in specific national environments and by broader developments at a global level.

It is pertinent to note here that Alastair Bonnett's detailed overview of antiracism in the second half of the twentieth century highlighted this complex diversity of ideas and movements that were seen collectively as part of the same phenomenon. In his typology of antiracisms, Bonnett helpfully breaks them down into various categories, including everyday antiracism, multicultural antiracism, psychological antiracism, radical antiracism, anti-Nazi antiracism and representational antiracism (Bonnett 2000). In addition to this typology, Bonnett's account also focuses on the dilemmas around antiracism in the context of discussions about the interrelationship between antiracist mobilizations and other mobilizations framed by feminism, ethnicity, white identities and essentialized identities. He argues forcefully that it is through the intersections with these other sites of mobilization over an extended period that the core ideas of antiracism were formed and re-formed. It is also important to note that Bonnett highlights the differences between national forms of antiracism, and also the importance of local cultures and traditions.

Although in Bonnett's typology these forms of antiracism were seen as part of the same broad phenomenon, it is also clear from his analysis that each type can take different forms depending on national traditions and different ways of seeing and talking about race and racism, both in politics and in civil society. Indeed, in the decades since Bonnett produced this typology, it could be argued that we have seen a kind of broadening out of forms of antiracism, which have been expressed on various scales, whether at the national, local or global levels.

Writing as he was at the end of the 1990s, Bonnett sought to produce a typology of the antiracisms that he saw as circulating in both scholarly and political circles at the time. In this sense, he captured not just the circulation of ideas about antiracism in the context of scholarly and research circles, but the ways in which societal mobilizations around antiracism came to the fore at the end of the twentieth century (Waters 2023). Although it could be argued that there is a need to adapt this typology to take account of the developments we have seen in the past three decades, the key point that Bonnett was seeking to make remains pertinent today – namely, that there are various forms of antiracism at work at any one point in time, and these often develop their own sensibilities and ideological reference points. Indeed, it is also relevant to note that antiracisms can take a range of forms both in terms of ideology and in relation to organizational structures. This has also been evident in the development of antiracist mobilizations and movements in the past three decades in a diverse range of societies (Ferguson 2023; O'Brien 2009; van Dijk 2021). Indeed, it is even more evident that, over the past two decades, we have seen a growing diversity of forms of mobilization, reflected both in different ideological influences and often in different overarching objectives about how to transform the bounds of racism and racial inequalities in contemporary societies.

In this rapidly evolving environment that is seeing the emergence of new forms of racism, it is important to question the notion of antiracism as a uniform set of ideological and political values. Rather, contemporary forms of antiracism can best be seen as a broad set of ideas, policies, and practices and mobilizations that address the everyday realities of the changing forms of racism and racialized inequalities that they seek to tackle. Although they are connected by a common concern to oppose and undermine racism and to address racialized inequalities and divisions, it is also clear that, as they have evolved and changed over the past few decades, they have taken on diverse forms. Just as the new racisms have evolved in different directions during this period, so have antiracist ideas and values (Bonnett 2000; 2022; Zamalin 2019). This has led in practice to the formation of new forms of antiracism both within specific societies and at the transnational level.

In some of the scholarship on antiracism, a broad distinction is drawn between *liberal* and *radical* forms. The first are seen as tied to ideas about the role of racism as linked to individuals, rather than broader social and economic processes (Joseph-Salisbury and Connelly 2021; Kundnani 2023). While this kind of distinction may have some heuristic value, it is also the case that such labels are not that helpful when it comes to analysing the diverse range of ideas and mobilizations under the banner of antiracism. Part of the problem with such binary constructions of antiracism is that they rely on a heroic version of political mobilizations around race in which 'liberal' is coded as bad and 'radical' is coded as good. Yet, in practice, part of the challenge we face is that there is often a messy coalition of organizations, and racial, ethnic and community groups that mobilize around key areas of concern to antiracist activists, such as cases of racial injustice, access to resources, migrant rights or specific issues such as police violence and deaths in custody. It is also evident that some of the mobilizations are framed around local issues and concerns, while others are framed symbolically around national and transnational concerns and preoccupations. Even campaigns on specific issues, such as police violence or harassment of minorities, are framed around a mixture of these mobilizations.

We should also recognize, as Bonnett and other scholars have emphasized, that ideologies about antiracism have not evolved in isolation from broader intellectual and political currents that came to the fore from the 1970s and 1980s onwards (Bonnett 2022; HoSang 2021). This included movements focused on race and ethnicity, but also wider debates about identities framed around feminism, racial and ethnic identity politics, and the emergence of debates about critical whiteness studies in the 1990s and the decades beyond. This has also become even more evident in the context of the ongoing conversations among both researchers and activists on such issues as critical race theory, intersectionality, decoloniality and racial capitalism. All of these strands of critical debate have intersected at various points with the continuing conversations about antiracist politics and mobilizations.

Whatever the merits of these efforts to frame the evolution of a diverse range of antiracisms over the past few decades, perhaps the key issues that we need to research further, both theoretically and empirically, are the processes that have helped to shape and influence the development of these antiracisms. It is important both to explore questions about the origins of these diverse types of mobilizations and to investigate their evolution and impact on society on various scales. There is evidence of growing bodies of scholarship that focuses on the origins and development of antiracist organizations and mobilizations, and these studies have at least begun to address the gap between theoretical conceptualizations of antiracism and the complex range of social and political movements on the ground that are engaged with the overarching aim of challenging and eliminating racism in the social and political world around us.

Given the developments in antiracist politics and policies over the past three decades, it is important to begin to address the reality that, in all likelihood, a broad range of antiracist mobilizations and initiatives are likely to be needed in order to bring about substantive changes in contemporary societies in terms of racial justice and equity. This is something that we shall return to at various points in this book, but we shall now move on to explore the evolution of various forms of antiracism.

Evolution of antiracism

As we have already seen, an important component of contemporary antiracisms is framed around the recognition of the increasingly multicultural and diverse realities of societies and localities around us. Through much of the second half of the twentieth century and this century, processes of migration and minority formation have helped to fundamentally transform societies across Europe and North America in terms of how questions about race and equity are seen. An important facet of the emergence and evolution of antiracism can be traced to the development of policy agendas that sought to address racialized inequalities and divisions in the wider society. There have been various phases of policy response over this extended period, often linked to changing patterns of migration and racial formation, but also often interlinked to broader social and political transformations in the wider social environments. In the context of British society, for example, the genesis of these policy agendas can be traced back to the articulation of policies framed by ideas about multiculturalism from the 1960s to the 1980s and beyond (Bebber 2019). In areas such as education, housing, policing and employment, this was the period that saw the emergence of agendas that sought to address the everyday realities of racial, ethnic and cultural diversities in the wider society.

The ways in which these policy agendas dealt with issues of race, culture and difference have taken a number of forms from the second half of the twentieth century to the present. When the recognition of cultural difference defined the parameters of multiculturalism, the focus for what became known as antiracism was the concept of racism and processes of discrimination. Race equality rather than cultural awareness lay at the heart of antiracism as a policy approach and political aim. In the political environment of the late twentieth century, this converged with an emergence of identity politics in which the older class-based politics gave way to a vocal, active, high-profile social movement-driven agenda based around issues of gender, sexuality and race, which became known as new social movements.

Through much of the last two decades of the twentieth century and into this century, many of the most contentious debates about radical antiracist policies were seen in the context of local state politics. This became evident in the 1980s and 1990s in the UK when, during a long period of Conservative administrations that did not show much interest in tackling issues around racial inequalities, the pursuit of antiracist policies became a feature of local politics. Local authorities that were controlled by the Labour Party in areas such as London, and urban conurbations such as Manchester, the West Midlands and Sheffield, were seen through this period as leading the search for more radical policy agendas aimed at tackling racialized inequalities in areas such as employment, housing and education. This highlighted the complex ways in which the local is often the site of mobilizations around issues of antiracism, particularly in areas where the political voice and community mobilizations of minority communities had impacted on local political institutions through representation and electoral politics. The role of local politics in shaping anti-racism was not by any means a uniquely British phenomenon. Similar trends began to emerge in urban politics in European cities and regions, and even more so in the context of the United States and Canada.

The growing evidence of racism and the activism and lobbying of community-based groups showed that exclusion from and discrimination in key services and resources such as housing, education, health and employment was reaching a critical point. This was compounded by problems with the policing of black and minority communities and, in terms of local politics, by a chronic under-representation of black and ethnic minority politicians and employees in local government structures.

It is also the case that antiracist strategies and policies were not necessarily connected to state institutions. During the late twentieth century and the first decades of the twenty-first, local authority, community and third-sector organizations played a key role in developing a raft of initiatives specifically aimed at delivering equal opportunities and equal outcomes in relation to race and ethnicity (Becker 2021; Ferguson 2023; Paul 2020). We saw this process in the ways that positive action initiatives and target commitments for black and ethnic minority recruitment and representation were commonly adopted by organizations and radical local authorities. The need to have ethnic monitoring procedures in terms of access to and allocation of social goods became a widely accepted norm and the collection of data relating to ethnicity, gender and sexuality gradually became a standard aspect of routine activities such as applying for jobs, employee profiling, health service provision and experience, housing and policing services and so forth (Back, Keith, Shukra and Solomos 2023). While energies went into the technical collection of these forms of data, what then happened to it in terms of using it to interpret the fairness, success or otherwise of policies was more uncertain. But the pressure to address inequalities and to provide evidence that progress was being achieved did emphasize the visibility of race equality issues in social policy.

Part of the push for antiracist policies and initiatives can be traced to research agendas that revealed black and ethnic minority under-representation in employment, higher education, public and private-sector organizations, and cultural institutions. It was partly on the basis of this research that we saw through the 1980s and 1990s a series of policy interventions such as specialist advisors on race; a review of job specifications, job selection and promotion criteria; and efforts to attract more black and minority candidates by advertising positions in black and ethnic minority media. It is also in this period that we saw a growth in race and cultural awareness training for employees, and particularly those involved in human resources and recruitment.

At the same time, many organizations, local authorities and government bodies established race units and race committees, declared themselves equal opportunities employers, and made discrimination and racism disciplinary offences in the workplace. Race hatred and racist violence became a focus of concern in housing departments, particularly in authorities with significant black and ethnic minority populations. Local authorities pressured police to tackle racial harassment, and racial harassment policies became part of tenancy agreements and meant that tenants could now be evicted for race hate behaviour. Consultation with, and the participation of, local black and ethnic minority communities became a key activity for organizations with an antiracist approach. This commitment saw black activists co-opted onto a range of committees in education, health, housing, leisure and policing, and the establishment of consultative forums across a range of issues, from young people and the arts to health and the elderly.

Not all of these initiatives were taken under the umbrella of antiracism, not least because it was still the case that antiracism was often associated broadly with the politics of the left. But the development of this range of initiatives at the end of the twentieth century and into the present highlighted the ways in which broader ideas about racial justice and equality had come to the fore both in public organizations and in large swathes of private-sector corporations in this period.

Indeed, an important facet of some of these initiatives was that the focus remained very much on the need to remedy racism through forms of race awareness and diversity training that were squarely focused on the individual, particularly those in positions of authority. It was in this context that we saw the emergence and development of forms of race awareness training that were aimed at teaching individual street-level bureaucrats the language of race consciousness and in changing their perceptions of racial differences and identities (Bourne 2016; Katz 1978). This strand of work became the subject of intense debate, in the context of both national and local politics. It also became the site of conflict and tension about the extent to which race awareness training represented an ideology that questioned dominant values in education and society (Palmer 1986).

A related development through the 1990s and 2000s saw the growth of an identifiable core of *race experts* who were seen as providing a route towards training bureaucrats and corporate decision-makers in questions about race and ethnicity. It was in this environment that scholars such as Elizabeth Lasch-Quinn began to talk about the rise of a kind of therapeutic form of new age thinking about racism, often also linked to the development of strategies for implementing new understandings of race in organizational settings (Lasch-Quinn 1996; 2001). Critics such as Lasch-Quinn saw the influence of this new age race thinking as leading to a situation where much of the attention was on the role of *race experts* and their therapeutic strategies, rather than efforts to address the structural roots of racism in society.

Bearing these limitations in mind, it is important to note that the reach of antiracism extended to local geographies, as streets, squares, public buildings and estates were renamed in efforts to reflect Britain's multicultural and colonial past and present. Some organizations adopted all of these strategies, others were more partial, but what is notable is the visibility of these initiatives within the public sphere. Some of this visibility was in the everyday environment. For example, Paul Gilroy highlights an early campaign in London by the Greater London Council to declare 'London Against Racism' and 'London as an Anti-Racist Zone'. As part of this campaign, a series of billboard adverts appeared which each carried strap lines such as 'If you're not part of the solution you're part of the problem' and 'When racism stops you being efficient are you doing your job?' (Gilroy 1987: 142, 147). Such campaigns sought to highlight the social and economic harm caused by racism and the need for antiracist strategies to help produce a different social reality.

Although Gilroy is referring to campaigns that were current in the 1980s and 1990s, it is interesting to note that similar ideas and campaigns are still being pursued into the present. During the public debates about Brexit in 2015 and 2016, the response of the Mayor of London and other local politicians was to launch a campaign that drew on the idea of London as an *open city*, and to emphasize its cosmopolitan character, its diversity, its cultural and social ties to the world and its openness to strangers and others (Georgiou 2017; Yazici et al. 2023). Again, this campaign was underpinned by a number of symbolic messages about London being a diverse and open city, a city of settlement and sanctuary, and at some level composed of something more than the sum of its diverse components. In framing the diversities in London as part of its identity, an element of the focus of the mayor of London, along with other local politicians, was to emphasize the idea that, even after the separation from broader European policies after Brexit, there was a need to keep the city open and involved in wider processes.

Through much of the period at the end of the twentieth century, antiracism became part of an intensely mediated and intensely political environment as the acrimonious battlegrounds between local and national politics were struggled over and as national identity and access to social goods and equal service delivery were campaigned and fought for. Looking back at this period, it is clear that the gains achieved by the various antiracist strategies and initiatives adopted in the 1980s and 1990s were not always sustained in the longer term. But it is clear that the period constituted an extraordinary policy moment in which politics, dissent, race, social justice, anxiety, social change, and formal processes and community-based campaigns and interventions converged and became deeply entangled. Antiracism as a policy trope tapped directly into the big questions of disadvantage, discrimination, exclusion, marginalization and racism, and did so by mobilizing uncomfortable and challenging sets of issues relating to power and subordination. This meant that antiracism was never going to have an easy passage or affectionate place in the public domain. Some of this is reflected in the media relationship to antiracism and its deeply acrimonious nature, and in the nature of the opposition from the political right to the antiracist policy interventions made by some municipal policy makers.

In terms of redistribution of social goods and equal access to services, and the opening up of processes and procedures, then antiracist policy interventions did have an impact. In this context, it is possible to see that antiracist initiatives put race onto the policy agenda and they did so in a new and very different language from previous policy approaches to race and multiculture. They ushered in new policy procedures around fair and equal access, delivery, allocation, recruitment, selection and promotion; and they established new policy architectures such as race committees, advisors, units; they led to increased numbers of black and ethnic minority local authority employees in areas that had been previously exclusively white, and established lines of consultation with black and ethnic minority groups and communities and organizations.

Antiracism as a policy approach was constantly fraught and uneven in terms of its successes. In his critique of municipal antiracism, Paul Gilroy has highlighted the crude essentialism through which race and the social relations that it helps to shape are overwhelmingly conceived. In developing his critical analysis of antiracism, Gilroy argues:

> 'Race' is, after all, not the property of powerful, prejudiced individuals but an effect of complex relationships between dominant and subordinate social groups [. . .] Even within a single social formation at a particular phase of its development racism will not be an unbroken continuous presence. It will be unevenly developed. Even where it is diffuse it will never be uniform. The different forces which form 'races' in concrete political antagonisms will operate at differing tempos and in contrasting ways according to immediate circumstances. Racial attacks may be higher in one area than the next. (Gilroy 1987: 149)

For Gilroy, the efforts to counter racism and deliver a different approach to multiculture are too essentially and bureaucratically formed and framed to be able to effectively cope with the highly contingent, always in flux and intensely complex formations that racism helps to produce, at the level of both the nation and the locality.

While this is an important point, and one with which I agree, I would also suggest that the efforts to create an agenda and a set of interventions to confront and address racism in this period were significant, both at the end of the twentieth century and into the 2000s and 2010s. This resulted in intense debates and conversations about both the meaning of anti-racism and the wider forms of diversity that were evident in societies such as Britain, the United States and more generally. This intensity, along with its conceptual limits, meant that anti-racism, as a policy strategy, was always likely to be uneven in its impact on key institutions in the wider society. This became evident in the public conversations that took place in the early

2000s around the report of the Commission on the Future of Multi-Ethnic Britain, which was chaired by Bhikhu Parekh and included critical scholars such as Stuart Hall among its members (Parekh 2000). The response to the report of the commission served to highlight tensions between liberal and radical perspectives on how best to respond to ethnic and racial diversities, and it also signalled some of the tensions that were to come to the fore in the following decades (Favell 2001; McLaughlin and Neal 2007). But, at the same time, the underlying vision articulated in the report – of a Britain that was increasingly multi-ethnic – can be seen, in hindsight at least, as an effort to push back at those who were holding on to a vision of Britain as still essentially white and monocultural.

By the 1990s and 2000s, explicit commitment to antiracism had waned and most local authorities, experiencing a variety of restructuring and reorganization of key services away from local authority control, retreated from antiracist-influenced policy interventions. But it is a rather strange paradox that the antagonisms and divisiveness that appeared to characterize antiracism still managed to deliver a form of policy consensus nevertheless. This consensus was sanitized in that the more radical, social justice thinking of antiracism was marginalized.

Throughout this period, antiracism remained at best a contradictory phenomenon. While antiracists prioritized race and raised expectations about the possibilities of change, antiracist policy interventions had at best a limited impact on national and local policy agendas, leading to a situation where the impact of policy interventions continued to be seen as rather limited or sometimes dismissed as inconsequential.

Politics, antiracism and resistance

As I have argued already, it is important, particularly in the contemporary environment, to locate antiracism within a broader politics that involves efforts to resist racism and move beyond it. We have seen important political mobilizations around questions of race and racism over the second half of the twentieth century and into the present, and it is against the broader background of these mobilizations that contemporary antiracisms have emerged and taken root in the world around us.

It is important to note here that, in the context of political and social movement mobilizations over the past few decades, a recurrent demand has been the call for racialized minorities to gain better access to the institutions of political representation and power. This call for greater representation has been evident both in the formal political sphere and in mobilizations in transitional and alternative political and community-based organizations. But, beyond the issue of representation and inclusion, an underlying concern has been how to ensure that increased levels of representation can lead to a shift in relations of power both in the political sphere and in the wider society. This concern for greater representation is premised on the broad idea that it is only through such a process of inclusion that racial and ethnic minorities will be able to help shape policies that address racial injustice as well as other structural inequalities. There have been some positive shifts in levels of minority representation in political institutions over the past few decades, but an ongoing area of debate has focused on how far this increased level of representation has in turn impacted on policy and political agendas (Back, Keith, Shukra and Solomos 2023). Indeed, in much of the critical scholarship on this issue, a recurrent theme has been the argument that there remains a major gap in terms of policies that address the structural forms of racial inequality in contemporary societies.

At the same time, it needs to be emphasized that political debates about antiracism have developed not just in the context of North America and Europe but increasingly on a global scale. Much of the emerging scholarship on antiracism has highlighted the ways in which, over the past few decades, efforts to tackle racism have taken shape on a global scale. Teun A. van Dijk has analysed the evolution and transformation of antiracist political and civil society discourses in Brazil, and argued forcefully that the long history of resistance to racism and its institutions lies at the heart of the development of both antiracist discourses and practices (van Dijk 2020). It is also interesting to note in this context that the account of antiracism that van Dijk and others have outlined in relation to Brazil can be broadened to take account of trends and developments in Latin America more generally (Moreno Figueroa and Wade 2022), since in recent times there have been important transformations in the conversations about both racisms and antiracisms across the continent.

The example of Brazil is important to include in any rounded analysis of antiracism as a globalized phenomenon, but it also clear that questions about antiracism are coming to the fore in other geopolitical contexts outside of the environs of the Global North. In the context of the end of the twentieth century and the current period, mobilizations about racism became an important feature of Brazilian politics. It led to the development of both national and more localized efforts to challenge the silences about racism that have characterized earlier periods (Hamilton et al. 2001; Silva 2022).

But it is equally important to include the long histories of antiracism in the context of South Africa, which were central to its development through the long twentieth century and into the period of the apartheid regime. Through much of this history, there were ongoing processes of resistance to the structures of racial domination that became an entrenched part of the realities of South Africa both before and after the formal establishment of the apartheid state. Indeed, much of this pattern of resistance and opposition to racism helped to shape the ideologies of other social movements across the globe. It has also become evident that, even in the context of the creation of the new political realities of post-apartheid South Africa, questions about racism and antiracism remain a core issue both socially and politically (Comaroff 1998; Fredrickson 1998; Levenson and Paret 2023). In a broader sense, the histories of ideologies of resistance to racism in South Africa have become part of the ideological discourse about antiracism on a global scale.

In the context of the past two decades, the mobilizations framed around Black Lives Matter in the United Sates and at a broader global level have also helped to highlight the ways in which antiracist mobilizations are both responsive to specific issues and at the same time often seek to address wider questions about the structural basis of racism and racialized inequalities in contemporary societies. Much of the scholarship on Black Lives Matter has picked up on the mix of political and social movement ideas that have come together to shape the approach of activists who have become involved in the movement, particularly in the United States (Hesse and Hooker 2017; Hooker 2017; Lebron 2017; Makalani 2017; Tillery 2019). In this sense, it is a movement that includes ideas and values linked to antiracism, but it is also influenced and shaped by ideas and values linked to black feminism, environmentalism and anti-capitalism.

Another important thread in antiracist mobilizations in recent years has been the various efforts to address the legacies of colonialism and imperialism as they are represented and commemorated in contemporary societies. As scholarship and research have begun to explore the connections between the long histories of slavery and colonialism and our cities, economies, educational and cultural institutions, there has been a growing awareness that mobilizations about memorials linked to slavery in the United States, and colonialism in the case of movements such as Rhodes Must Fall, have helped to emphasize the continuing mobilizing power of the signifier of race within political cultures and in civil society (Frank and

Ristic 2020; Hayward, Threadcraft, Lebron and Shelby 2019; Shepherd 2020). Indeed, part of the impact of these kinds of debates about historical memory and its representation in the form of statues and museums has been to bring questions about racism and colonialism into the public sphere in ways that we have not witnessed before.

In the past few decades, we have seen both consistent pressure for greater diversity in political institutions and efforts to address the under-representation of racial and ethnic minorities within political parties, representative bodies and political institutions. Over the past decade, these pressures have become even more intense as mobilizations around a range of issues have become an important feature of political debate. An overview of trends and developments in Britain in relation to political mobilizations has highlighted the complex range of issues that have come together to shape the contemporary situation:

> We have also witnessed the emergence of new and significant progressive movements such as Black Lives Matter, Rhodes Must Fall, various Decolonial initiatives and the formation of refugee support networks and others. While these, like the particular forms of racism to which they respond, are new they must be understood both sociologically and historically in terms of the historical precedents, legacies and projects they reference or are implicated in or cut off from. (Bhattacharyya, Virdee and Winter 2020: 1–2)

This is an important point that needs to be borne in mind in any rounded analysis of this area since, in practice, we need also to understand that political mobilizations often work across a complex web of issues that have resonance in national, local and transnational political spheres. It also signals the way in which contemporary mobilizations for political representation and inclusion are often linked with broader historical as well as contemporary questions. As scholarship on Black Lives Matter has emphasized, although it is very much a product of the present environment, activists who are involved in the movement often make connections to broader historical issues such as slavery, colonialism, apartheid and other forms of segregation, as well as other types of racialized capitalism and domination (Lebron 2017; Olney 2021; Tillery 2019).

Underlying these theoretical and historical controversies, however, are more practical questions about the relationship between black and ethnic minority political mobilization and other forms of politics, based on gender and class. This theme is central, for example, in the controversies surrounding the processes of political exclusion and inclusion that have shaped the experiences of black and ethnic minority communities in a wide variety of national contexts. It has been a recurrent theme in debates that go back to the formation of pressure groups and political movements that sought to influence the Labour Party during the 1980s and 1990s to take the question of minority representation more seriously. Similar questions have been raised over the years about the development of black politics in the US, particularly during the period from the 1960s to the 1970s, in the aftermath of the Civil Rights Movement and the voting rights reforms that sought to open the political sphere to minority representation. In addition, during the late 1960s and 1970s, the mobilizations inspired by the Black Panthers became an important means of political organization, both in terms of mainstream politics and at the level of local communities. As Alondra Nelson has highlighted in her study of the efforts by the Black Panther Party to tackle medical and other forms of inequality and discrimination in poor black communities, one of the major successes of the movement was the product of its efforts to tackle the impact of poverty in areas such as health and food poverty (Nelson 2011). By mobilizing in a wide range of poor urban neighbourhoods around these issues, the Panthers were able to garner support and sympathy across a cross-section of the communities and to highlight the need for autonomous political mobilization to raise the profile of key issues faced by these communities. There are still, however, few studies of black and minority politicians at both the national and the local scale, the impact of minority participation on policy agendas and access to resources, and detailed studies of political movements and ideologies. Such issues have been the subject of detailed research within the context of American political science and sociology, however, where there has been much more detailed empirical research on the evolving dynamics of race and ethnic political mobilizations (Brown 2014; Gaines 1996; King and Smith 2011; McClain and Johnson 2018; McClain and Tauber 2018). Whatever the gaps and limitations of research agendas in relation to the role of race and ethnicity, there is little doubt that during this early part of the twenty-first century racialized political mobilizations have become an important site of contestation both within and outside the mainstream political sphere. Indeed, during the past decade, mobilizations around Black Lives Matter and related issues have done much to bring this dimension of the current situation to the forefront of contemporary political discussions as well as scholarly research agendas (Francis and Wright-Rigueur 2021; Lopez Bunyasi and Smith 2019; Scott and Brown 2016; Tillery 2019). These bodies of scholarship have begun to address a number of important gaps in the analysis of political mobilizations by black and minority communities and to provide insights into the ways in which these mobilizations are reshaping the political agendas of antiracism. It is to this issue that we now turn.

Rethinking the politics of antiracism

I have argued in this chapter that we are at a new turning point in the politics of racism and antiracism. In the contemporary environment of the early twenty-first century, we need to develop critical research agendas that ask questions about the possibilities for radical antiracist strategies and policies in key social arenas in our societies. Just as the period from the 1950s to the 1970s represented a period of sustained, and sometimes successful, efforts to challenge racism and racialized inequalities (Banton 1974), we need to think more about the kind of research agendas and conversations that can help us make sense of the current period. After a period of retreat and silence on issues of antiracism and racial justice at the end of the twentieth century, the past three decades have seen renewed debates and conversations about the next steps that we need to take if we are going to move towards racial justice and equity. The coming period is likely to see even more intense discussion about these issues, particularly as we see the emergence of new forms of both racist and antiracist mobilizations in the world around us.

This process of renewal and contestation became evident initially in the United States, but these debates have also begun to shape political and policy debates in Europe, Latin America, Australasia and at a broader global level in the past two decades as well.

As we have seen in this chapter, what these debates have helped to highlight is that there is a need for a serious and nuanced conversation about the kinds of antiracist strategies and policies we need that will be relevant to the present. In addition to this key point, we have engaged with an important challenge that needs to be part of ongoing conversations in the coming period – namely, how to develop a scholarly and policy agenda that can set out practical programmes that challenge racism and racial inequalities. Rather than seeing progress towards futures shaped by antiracist ideas and values in simple binary terms that are premised on the idea of progress in absolute terms, I have argued that any progress in this field is likely to be uneven. This requires a questioning of absolutist dismissals of what antiracism has managed to achieve over the past few decades and the development of an antiracist imagination that allows for action against racism on various fronts, including mobilizations within institutions, a politics of refusal and protest, and everyday forms of resistance and efforts to remedy and challenge entrenched forms of inequality and division.

In highlighting the need for these critical conversations going forwards, part of the challenge we face is to question the widespread patterns of denial about the realities of racial inequalities and racism in our societies. As a number of scholars have argued, an important facet of contemporary efforts to see societies as becoming increasingly *post-racial* necessarily involves a denial of the complex histories of racism over the past few centuries and more, as well as a silence on the continuing impact of these historical processes on the present. David Goldberg captures the ways in which denial and erasure are at the heart of post-racial political and social imaginaries, when he points out that: 'The postracial denies the historical conditions and their legacy effects. It buries, alive, those very conditions that are the grounds of its own making. Buried alive, those conditions continue to constitute a hold, a handicap, a disability at the intersection of race and class on those forced to bear their load' (Goldberg 2015: 76).

The processes of erasure and denial described by Goldberg have, if anything, progressed even further in the period since. Indeed, an important part of mobilizations over the past decade and more has been focused on efforts to question the erasure of the ways in which racialized inequalities persist and impact on the everyday experiences of racialized minorities in the present.

An interesting example of these processes of denial and silence can be found in the fraught discussions in the United States and beyond about the issue of reparations for slavery and racialized exclusion. While public discourses about restitutions have been part of both scholarly and political debates for some time, they have taken on a more contested and intense form in the contemporary environment. The contested nature of debates about reparations has been highlighted in Marcus Hunter's critical analysis of conversations about recompense in American society, where he explores the ways in which an open and radical agenda for implementing reparations can become part of a process for 'healing the soul' of American society. A particular strength of Hunter's account can be found in the way he helpfully highlights the often messy silences that haunt efforts to develop strategies of reparation that speak to both the past and the present of racial division and inequality. He goes on to argue:

> Until we live in a world where it is safe to advocate for peace without fear of death or defamation while being Black and affirm the Black experience while challenging racial capitalism and white supremacy, we must collectively work together, support, and love on each other to ensure that in our lifetime systemic racism and inequality are counterbalanced by systemic equity, systemic inclusivity, and systemic shared human value and dignity. To achieve that world, we need radical reparations, a dynamically implemented and imagined set of repairs and renovations that by robustly addressing the sins of the past unlock the path to a freer, safer, and more just society. There are piles of injuries to repair. And these piles must be sorted to reveal all the forms of reparations needed. (Hunter 2024: 313)

Although the very notion of *radical reparations* outlined by Hunter is intensely contested by large swathes of American society, particularly those who see themselves as on the radical right, he suggests that there is much to be gained if there is an open conversation about reparations and racial justice. In particular, he argues that the challenge faced in the contemporary period is how to bring about substantive change through racial healing, repair and equity and create the new society that was promised but not delivered at the end of slavery.

Although somewhat more specific than the call made by Hunter for a programme of radical reparations at a societal level, recent mobilizations about the policing of racialized minorities in both the US and Europe have also drawn attention to the need to develop a clearer research understanding of the bureaucratic and everyday processes that help to shape street-level interactions between the police and racialized minorities. In discussing an empirically focused research project on antiracist mobilizations about police violence in France, Magda Boutros argues that there is a need to locate contemporary mobilizations about this issue within a broader historical narrative about colonialism and racialization:

> My findings suggest that making connections between the racial past and present provides a resource to move beyond individualist understandings of racism and to highlight how colonially constituted state structures maintain and reinforce racial inequalities. They also show that striving to gain access to state records can allow activists to uncover specific institutional policies that lead to disparate outcomes, and to pinpoint the political, economic, and social power relations shaping these policies, and their effects on street-level interactions between the police and racialized populations. (Boutros 2024: 14–15)

For Boutros, and other scholars, it is precisely the need to explore the changing historical dynamics that underpin such phenomena as police violence against racial minorities that will allow antiracist activists to develop strategies for changing institutions from within. In making this point, these scholars are not merely using historical patterns of racialization as a point of reference, but arguing that it is only through rigorous research in the archives that we can recover the complex histories of racialization with regard to policing and related issues.

We should remember, too, that the various forms of antiracism that have evolved, both historically and in the present, do not exhaust the possible avenues for challenging racism as it shapes different political cultures and landscapes in the world around us. Just as a focus on the US or on the situation in various European countries is not sufficient to allow us to think about the politics of challenging racism as a global phenomenon, it remains important to think beyond frameworks that have been shaped by specific historical realities and to grapple with the changing politics of racism in different parts of the globe.

At a broader level, it is important to look closely at the ways in which the transition from ideas about antiracism to putting them into practice involves a clear understanding of the workings of racism, in both its structural and individual forms. We shall return to these issues in the next chapter as we explore the routes taken to put antiracist strategies and policies into practice.

3

From Theory to Practice

Chapters 1 and 2 have been focused on a critical discussion of the evolution and changing forms of antiracism, both from a historical angle and over the past few decades. I now want to move to a critical discussion of efforts to put antiracism into practice at various levels in contemporary societies. The main areas we shall discuss in this chapter are the place of antiracism in civil society as well as local and national state institutions, and efforts to develop antiracist practices in both the public and private sectors. Given this focus we shall draw on examples from specific policy arenas as well as the role of legislation in framing the direction of policies aimed at tackling forms of racism and racial discrimination in specific institutional contexts and in society more generally. At the same time, we shall also discuss the possibilities for bringing about change through everyday forms of antiracist practice and the formation of alliances that bring people together across racial, gender and class boundaries.

Given the key concerns of this book, we shall be concentrating in this chapter on efforts to put antiracism into practice over the past few decades. I am aware that there is a longer-term history to such efforts, both during the nineteenth century and through much of the twentieth. The lengthy struggles against institutionalized segregation in South Africa and the United States for much of the twentieth century are examples of this longer-term background, and indeed these struggles remain an important point of reference through to the present (Baker 1993; Cell 1982; Fredrickson 1981). It is also evident that the decades that helped to shape the Civil Rights Movement in the United States – namely, the period from the 1950s to the 1970s – did much to influence contemporary discussions about the politics of antiracism. But it is perhaps during the last few decades of the twentieth century and the beginning of the twenty-first that we have begun to see a renewed conversation about what it is that we mean by the notion of putting antiracist policies into practice, in the forms of strategies for changing society or specific institutions.

In developing this analysis, we shall also be laying the foundations for the critical discussion of the changing conversations about antiracism in the current environment that will be the main focus of chapters 4 and 5.

Movements, ideas, policies

At the heart of antiracism today, there are movements and ideologies that seek to challenge the pervasiveness of racism and its impact on social and political institutions in our societies. This is a key point made by those researchers who have sought to provide an analysis of the evolving forms of antiracism in the contemporary conjuncture. In linking core antiracist arguments to pressure to change policy and political agendas, an underlying issue that is being discussed is the question of how to move from ideas about antiracism to practical policy agendas that can impact on the social world and change it.

In this context, it important to remember a distinction made by David Goldberg between what he terms *responsive antiracism* and *ecological antiracism*. The first type of antiracism is seen as largely responsive to events and actions that are expressions of racism in the present. By contrast, *ecological antiracism* seeks to 'address the larger landscape of structural conditions supporting and enabling the reproduction of racist arrangements and expression' (Goldberg 2015: 168). From this perspective, struggles to transform structural inequalities based on race and ethnicity in areas such as employment, health, education, politics and criminal justice form part of *ecological antiracism*, in the sense that they seek to challenge entrenched inequalities in the wider society. The key point that Goldberg is making here is that responsive antiracism is very much shaped by the present and by events, but there is also a need for an antiracist perspective that looks to the question of how we can transform structural inequalities.

The argument that underpins this distinction is a valuable one, not least because it picks up on a tension that has been at the heart of antiracist mobilizations over the past few decades. But it is also clear that, when we look at efforts to put antiracism into practice, there is often a mix of both *responsive* and *ecological* concerns that are part of the everyday realities of antiracist mobilizations. This is particularly the case when we move away from looking at antiracisms from the top and see how antiracist mobilizations take shape through localized and community-based efforts to tackle the realities of racialized divisions and inequalities. From the perspective of activists involved in efforts to remedy particular injustices or issues, they are often focused on responding to immediate concerns, but they are also frequently aware of the broader context within which the immediate issues are located.

As I have argued already, much of the contemporary research on antiracism has highlighted the need to look beyond the mainstream political sphere to explore how more radical forms of antiracism can emerge and help to shape societies.

But, in addition, these bodies of research have forced onto scholarly and political agendas the question of how we can move from talking about the causes of racialized divisions to putting into practice strategies for translating ideas into practice. It is partly as a result of these ongoing conversations that we have seen increased attention to forms of radical antiracist movements and mobilizations outside of the mainstream political sphere. This has been brought much more to the fore in the past two decades by the development of mobilizations around Black Lives Matter, alongside other non-traditional movements focused on racial justice, and has highlighted the complex forms that political identities around racial and ethnic issues can take (Lopez Bunyasi and Smith 2019; Ostertag 2019; Thurston 2018). Indeed, perhaps the most important development we have seen during this period has been the growth of movements that see themselves as working largely outside of the mainstream institutional forms of political negotiation and bargaining. This is a choice by some of the radical movements that have come to the fore recently as a way to give voice to their frustration at the pace of change in making substantive progress in tackling the roots of racism in key areas of society.

This is a point that has been highlighted in Juliet Hooker's account of the impact of some of the mobilizations that took place against police violence against African Americans, and which eventually led to the formation of the Black Lives Matter movement. Hooker highlights a differentiation between black politics aimed at *descriptive representation* and a trend towards what she defines as *black political radicalization*. While this is quite a broad distinction, it helpfully puts centre stage the question of what representation actually means in practice. As Hooker argues, it is important to delve more fully into the issues that have helped to shape processes of radicalization over the past two decades as the racial divides in American society have become more evident:

The anti-police violence protests that erupted in Ferguson, Missouri, in 2014 and Baltimore in 2015, and the subsequent disproportionate police repression of citizen protesters, marked an important inflection point in US racial politics. The protests signaled a potential moment of black political radicalization, when pragmatic forms of black politics principally aimed at descriptive representation have been overshadowed by a vocal movement seeking to dismantle some of the key pillars of contemporary white supremacy: mass incarceration, violent policing, a biased criminal justice system, and the pervasive criminalization of black life. (Hooker 2017: 483–4)

In making this distinction between descriptive representation and black political radicalization, Hooker is suggesting that more radical strategies for change have emerged partly as a result of continuing frustration about the progress that has been achieved towards racial justice. She helpfully delineates a range of issues to do with racial injustice, in different social and political arenas, that remain unresolved even after the reforms that came into force in the 1960s and 1970s because of the mobilizations and counter-mobilizations that shaped much of the racial politics of American society during the 1950s and 1960s. These include underlying social divisions, economic and educational disparities, as well as questions about policing and criminal justice. It is precisely because these issues remain unresolved after this period, Hooker argues, that movements with a radical agenda for reform and structural change are gaining a voice both within the African American communities and among some sections of the wider society. At the same time, as other commentators have argued, this process of radicalization has also been met by a counter-politics that argues that the very demands for radical reform and racial justice are a threat to traditional American values (Smith and King 2024).

Although a number of these accounts are very much framed around the American context, it is also clear that in the broader global context we have seen a similar differentiation between modes of antiracist mobilization. This is why it is important to look at antiracist movements and mobilizations within a broader comparative analytical frame that includes the increasingly significant forms of black, ethnic and migrant political mobilization and resistance. It is perhaps not surprising that the focus is often on the United States, but we should also note that there has been considerable antiracist mobilization in Europe, Latin America and other regional environments. In practice, since the early 2000s, it has become evident that mobilizations by antiracist activists are often meshed together with political and community mobilizations on issues that concern not just race but other forms of social inequality and injustice. Such intermeshing of mobilizations does not necessarily lead to easy alliances between different groups, but it can be argued that it is through these efforts to connect different forms of struggle that we can begin to see possibilities for more radical change.

A key feature of the range of political mobilizations that have emerged and evolved in a range of directions at the beginning of the twenty-first century is that the demands for change are not always based simply on questions about race and ethnicity, since they are also often linked to broader issues of social justice. This is something that has attracted the attention of critical race scholars when they have sought to make sense of the political turbulence of the past two decades. Charles W. Mills, for example, has suggested that one way to make sense of recent antiracist political mobilizations is to see them from the perspective of an emergent *black radical liberalism* that seeks to provide an ideological frame for a politics of racial justice that brings together diverse social and political groups. Mills offers this proposal because he argues that liberalism has failed to address the realities of racism and racial injustice both historically and in the present (Mills 2017). Drawing on his broader analysis of the racial contract, Mills argues that a *deracialized liberalism* is needed, which combines the objective of achieving racial justice with a larger social justice politics that brings a concern to address the connections between racial, class and gender inequalities. Part of the difficulty, of course, is that the conditions for creating coalitions and alliances that can sustain a deracialized liberalism are not always obvious in many political environments, but the underlying arguments articulated by Mills and others remain an important challenge in the present political environment.

From this perspective, although it is important to centre the role of antiracist movements and ideologies within their own terms, in reality it is equally necessary to locate them within a broader set of mobilizations and struggles about inequality and justice in our contemporary social situation. We shall return to these issues in chapters 4 and 5, but the key point to make here is that, in the context of everyday concerns about inequality and injustice, there are real and substantive pressures to build alliances and to create spaces for the formation of common interests.

Antiracist policies and practices

As was argued in chapter 2, antiracist policies and practices over the past few decades have been uneven and often limited in terms of their impact on racism and racial inequalities. Part of the reason for this unevenness can be traced to the ways in which antiracist policies and practices have been and remain sites of dispute and contestation in many societies. At another level, part of the reason for the relative failures in antiracist policies can be traced to how they have been framed in such a way as to focus on tackling racism at an individual rather than a societal level. This is a point highlighted by David Goldberg when he argues: 'Racism is not only about what one person does to another. Racisms are always expressed within a landscape of racially framed and structured conditions. They exist in an ecology of power relations and racial conceptions ordered by that landscape. So every racism is relationally structured' (Goldberg 2015: 107).

For Goldberg, part of the reason for the relative failure of antiracism in practice can be traced to a failure to address the *ecology of power relations* and *racial conceptions* that have helped to maintain racial inequalities and resisted efforts to challenge their continued impact on social and political relations.

An important facet of contemporary black and minority political mobilizations has been framed by some commentators as an expression of forms of black diasporic mobilization. The work of Michael Hanchard has been important in terms of helping to develop our understanding of the changing forms of political mobilizations around racialized political identities (Gooding-Williams, Goldberg, Hooker and Hanchard 2020; Hanchard 2010; 2018). Aside from his interventions in a wide range of theoretical debates, he has been closely involved in carrying out research in the United States and Brazil, as well as trying to develop a comparative frame for the analysis of race and political mobilization. What is particularly important about Hanchard's research in this area is that he has managed to weave together an analytical frame that focuses attention both on the efforts to transform the mainstream political spheres in countries such as the United States and Brazil, and on the struggles that have been shaped by the actions of social movements and actors that seek to give voice to those who have been systematically excluded from political life over long historical periods. In his study of the historical and contemporary relationship between race and democracy, he argues that 'The spectre of difference has hovered over democratic polities ranging from classical Athens to contemporary nation-states. The fear, the fright of difference is only unknown to those who have not been paying attention' (Hanchard 2018: 207).

Hanchard's overarching argument about the linkages between fears around race and around difference helpfully highlights both the historical roots of contemporary divisions and the continuing relevance of racialized inequalities in shaping democratic institutions, even at a time when many nation-states have a formal commitment to the values of equality and difference. It is also worth noting his continued emphasis on the importance of doing research on the comparative politics of race, since often one of the limitations of research on race and politics is the absence of a comparative analytical frame.

Efforts to lay the foundations for doing comparative research on the politics of racism and antiracism are important since this brings to the fore the need to explore the dynamics of mobilizations at different scales. In previous research on the changing forms of minority political mobilizations, emphasis has been placed on the need for detailed research at the local, national and transnational levels in order to gain a broader vision of how the politics of race and ethnicity speaks simultaneously to the politics of recognition that demands visibility of the racial or ethnic political subject and to the universal demand to be treated equally, with difference between individuals anonymized or erased (Back, Keith, Shukra and Solomos 2023). Yet, it has also been emphasized that it is important to bear in mind the ways in which in practice black and ethnic minority political mobilizations in the late twentieth and early twenty-first century often combine different interests and demands, and do so in ways that are difficult to unravel in practice. We need, nevertheless, to discuss how we can bring an understanding of the changing dynamics of the politics of recognition and the politics of equality into the analysis of the social significance of race and ethnicity.

The importance of looking beyond the boundaries of nation states in this area is not in itself a new issue, since in many ways the mobilizations around the Civil Rights Movement and

Black Power in the 1960s and 1970s were often framed through a transnational lens (Narayan 2019; Ogbar 2019; Slate 2012a; 2012b). But, as mobilizations under the banner of Black Lives Matter have emphasized, there is a very clear effort in the contemporary environment to frame struggles for inclusion and black empowerment on a global scale. Barnor Hesse and Juliet Hooker take this point a step further when they draw attention to what they see as a process of deterritorialization in forms of contemporary black political mobilizations:

> At the same time, we need to think about different political forms of blackness as deterritorialization. This involves the creative disembedding of meanings of black solidarity from local events and settings, where these meanings become transferable to other places, linking previously disparate black communities in affinity and dialogical networks of discourses and activities. Since 2014 this political dynamic of territorialization and deterritorialization has increasingly become a mainstay in the proliferation of mobilizations against the violence of racial policing across the black diaspora under the political slogan 'Black lives matter'. (Hesse and Hooker 2017: 444)

In making the linkages between the local, national and transnational forms of mobilization, Hesse and Hooker are also drawing attention to the need for a detailed analysis of the complex connections between disparate black communities and the possibilities for linking their struggles together. Given the important mobilizations that have emerged in various contexts over the past decade, it will be important to see how far-reaching the impact of such struggles will be in the coming period.

Changing racial orders

At a broad level, it can be argued that the underlying concern of efforts to put antiracism into practice involves attempts to challenge and change existing racial orders that have been shaped by both historical and contemporary processes. But the mechanisms for changing racial orders are complex and often involve both struggles within and outside of the dominant racial orders in a society. The ongoing debates about working within institutions to change them or pushing for change outside of the dominant power structures in a society reflect this uncertainty about how to bring about change, both within specific organizations and more generally in society. These debates are in a sense not surprising, since, as Caroline Knowles has shown, the formation of racial orders in a society is not a simple process and involves both structural patterns and everyday social interactions between individuals, communities and identities. For Knowles, racial orders 'are in fact composed of myriad and ordinary everyday social processes and mechanisms with which people interface in no predictable way' (Knowles 2003: 25). It is precisely this complexity and embeddedness of racial orders in social relations that makes it difficult to challenge and change them.

An interesting example of the workings of these complexities can be found in movements such as Black Lives Matter, and the forms that they have taken both in the United States and more globally. Although it is difficult to generalize from the experience of Black Lives Matter mobilizations, it is also important to note that when we look at the diverse range of interventions that go under this banner, they are not really a single movement with a fixed ideological frame. It is perhaps best seen as an alliance of diverse movements and interests that have coalesced around a wide range of issues. Among the issues that have been important in the mobilizations around Black Lives Matter, it has been noted that it has at various stages focused on police violence, but also on broader questions about reparations, black self-determination, community control and social justice. But among the movements that have worked under the banner of Black Lives Matter at various points, we have also seen an emphasis on broader social and political issues, including restructuring of the economy, and reforms in areas such as housing, education and healthcare (Smith and King 2021; 2024). Part of the concern of all these mobilizations is about the specific issues linked to policing and violence against racialized minorities, but at the same time they have made links to broader questions about racial and other forms of exclusion and injustice. In this sense, it is important to pay close attention to the complex ways in which the changing racial orders in the world around us are often shaped by a wide range of processes that are constantly evolving and changing in unpredictable ways.

Local and community mobilizations

It is also important to note that mobilizations at the local and community levels continue to play an important role. In the context of British society, for example, a number of studies have noted that everyday interventions about issues of concern within minority communities are an important form of political engagement around race and racism. Such mobilizations are often issue-centred and bring together both specific localized issues and broader questions about the role of the state and its institutions. One study focusing on campaigns around the issue of deaths in police custody over the past few decades points to the web of connections between localized concerns and broader mobilizations around Black Lives Matter as a key facet of these myriad actions:

The United Families and Friends Campaign (UFFC), a coalition of families from across the country campaigning for justice for loved ones killed in state custody, was an important presence at the BLM protests, and a key site of political education. UFFC, which holds a protest march on the last Saturday of October every year, is not a campaign that anyone chooses to join, but one that families and friends are forced to join when their loved ones are killed at the hands of the state. (Bhattacharyya et al. 2021: 195–6)

Similar trends have been evident in other contexts, with mobilizations focused on issues such as housing, school exclusions, policing and education often bringing together a complex web of organizations that have developed at both the local and the national scales. The development of such mobilizations is not in itself new, and indeed it is possible to trace out a broader history of both local and national mobilizations that are focused on these issues. But, by focusing attention on the complex forms of activity that have evolved in the contemporary environment, they do highlight the need to develop a more detailed understanding of the possibilities for radical change.

It is also important to analyse the role of antiracist mobilizations at different scales, from the national to the local. This will necessarily involve delving deeply into the comparative study of the politics of racism and trying to make sense of the continuing efforts to change the political and policy agendas from both within and without. We have suggested in another study of the changing politics of race that such a research strategy will of necessity need to mix conceptual analysis with empirical studies of the evolving political struggles to define and redefine political agendas and priorities (Back, Keith, Shukra and Solomos 2023). Although there have been some empirical studies of political mobilizations shaped by race and ethnicity, we still have few studies that seek to develop a comparative analytical frame that can allow us to explore differences and similarities between the local, national and transnational scales of political mobilization. There is therefore a need to develop this area of research by engaging more fully with developing more detailed studies of the political spaces in which struggles around race and ethnicity are going on in the contemporary environment. We have seen a broader literature on the importance of recognizing local histories and processes of community formation (Bloomfield 2019; Connell 2019; Perry 2016; Waters 2019) and, in the US context, we have a wealth of detailed studies of key cities and their political environment (Dawson 1994; Hooker 2016; King and Smith 2011). There is an urgent need to build on these studies and develop a comparative analysis of the changing position on race and ethnicity in political cultures and institutions.

One of the important lessons that we can take forwards from the contemporary environment is that there seems little doubt that the kinds of political and social movement mobilizations that have come to the fore over the past decade are likely to continue to play an important role in shaping the political agendas over the coming period. Whether it be issues such as the role of the police, access to employment and services, or access to education it is likely that issue-based mobilizations will remain an important site of contestation at different scales. An important open question about these movements is the impact they are likely to have in bringing about the kind of deracialized polity that will achieve equal access to political participation and representation for racialized communities in diverse societies. It is a question that is likely to remain both at the heart of scholarly research agendas and at the core of political mobilizations in the coming period.

The role of locally based antiracist alliances has been an important feature of these types of efforts to engage diverse communities with movements that seek to challenge entrenched power relations. For example, Ben-Tovim et al.

found that locally based antiracist alliances in Liverpool and Wolverhampton were doing much to promote minority political demands and mobilize opinion against racist organizations (Ben-Tovim, Gabriel, Law and Stredder 1986). From this, they concluded that, at the local level at least, antiracist political alliances remained an important part of the politics of racism in Britain. Furthermore, research carried out by Solomos and Back in Birmingham during the 1980s and 1990s revealed that coalition politics was doing much to shape minority political agendas during this period (Back and Solomos 1994; Solomos and Back 1995). While locally focused mobilizations do not in themselves have a direct impact on national policy and political agendas, they have over the years helped to shape some of the key features of antiracist politics and movements.

Everyday forms of antiracism

Alongside efforts to transform political and social institutions at a societal level or local level, it is also important to pay attention to the ways in which bottom-up everyday forms of antiracism have played an important role in tackling attitudes towards race, as well as in challenging racialized inequalities. Mobilizations that have focused on everyday expressions of racism are not in themselves new but they have come to the fore in recent years as a result of efforts by activists to draw attention to the need to tackle racism at all levels. This is evident across a broad range of European countries, but it is also clear from public policy debates in North America, Latin America, South Africa, and a few other parts of the globe that questions about everyday expressions of racism remain at the heart of continuing political and policy debates and conflicts (Bloch, Neal and Solomos 2013; Golash-Boza 2015; Solomos 2020). This perhaps explains why, alongside broader bodies of scholarship on antiracism, we have also seen in recent years growing bodies of research that address the phenomenon of everyday antiracism.

An interesting example of this body of work can be found in Kristine Aquino's extensive research among the Filipino diaspora in Australia. Aquino helpfully defines everyday antiracism and resistance as referring to the ways in which individuals, and communities, respond to racism and forms of exclusion in their everyday lives and spaces of encounter (Aquino 2017; 2020). She argues that such everyday forms of antiracism can include:

> The actions of victims confronting perpetrators, witnesses speaking out against racism, practices that bridge cultural difference, material and subjective strategies deployed by those on the receiving end of racism to repair stigmatized identities, and aestheticized expressions through popular culture such as forms of music, youth cultures and media that challenge racism. (Aquino 2020: 216)

From this perspective, these forms of antiracist mobilization are focused on helping to transform racism through creating forms of everyday interaction that leads to a questioning of racism within specific social, cultural and political environments.

This perhaps explains the growing interest among researchers, as well as antiracist activists, in looking at the possibilities for countering racism through popular culture, including music, art, sport and other cultural forms. In some ways, this is not a new phenomenon and has had a presence in antiracist mobilizations for some time. One historical example of efforts to develop antiracist political identities that drew upon the symbols of music and culture can be found in the efforts in the UK during the late 1970s and 1980s to oppose the increasing presence of neo-fascist groups that sought to mobilize on questions linked to race and immigration. A number of left-wing activist groups formed organizations such as the Anti-Nazi League and Rock Against Racism with the avowed aim of bringing together diverse groups around an agenda of countering the influence of neo-fascists among the young and other groups in the wider society. Such mobilizations took place both nationally and locally and brought together sections of the mainstream Labour Party, left-wing activists and black and ethnic minority organizations in order to oppose what they saw as their common enemy – namely, extreme right-wing racist political groups. Rock Against Racism, in particular, sought to counter the influence of the extreme right by bringing together activists and musical artists around the symbolic politics of shared musical and artistic values beyond the boundaries of race (McNeil 2023; Renton 2018).

But in recent years there has been renewed interest in this phenomenon as a specific expression of what Aquino and others have termed everyday antiracism. Efforts to focus antiracist values and ideas through visual culture, art and music have attracted particular attention in a range of different contexts (Frisina and Hawthorne 2017; Frisina and Kyeremeh 2022; Martiniello 2018). Although there is as yet not much detailed research on the workings of antiracism in the context of popular cultural forms such as music and art, there is at least a growing body of scholarship that explores the ways in which antiracist values and ideas have been popularized through everyday culture, particularly in the context of music. There are also some important ethnographic explorations of the ways in which questions of culture, race and generation interact in the formation of youth cultures and processes of racial and cultural formation. Camilla Hawthorne's exploration of these complex processes in the context of Italy (Hawthorne 2017; 2022), for example, is suggestive of the range of interactions in many local environments that help to shape these processes. What is particularly interesting about Hawthorne's research is the way she draws on extensive ethnographic research to explore the everyday processes that help to shape social and cultural interactions and lead to ongoing conversations about the role of race in the context both of youth cultures and of the wider society.

In some ways, this is not in itself a new phenomenon. Through much of the second half of the twentieth century and into the present, the role of popular music as a site for ongoing conversations about race and racism has been an important example of the ways in which changing ideas about race and racism are expressed. But perhaps what is somewhat new is that there has been an increasing focusing of attention on everyday cultural forms as a potential site for encouraging antiracist sensibilities and values. Rather than a focus on changing institutions, this focus on everyday forms of antiracism suggests that institutional changes need to be combined with efforts to see popular culture as a key site for challenging racist ideologies and values.

Another example of this kind of approach can be found in the area of sport. In the context of football, for example, we have seen a succession of initiatives, such as Kick it Out, that have sought to utilize fans' attachment to the sport and its cultural norms to challenge racism and popularize antiracist tropes (Penfold and Cleland 2022). Many of these initiatives seek not just to use professional football as a site for challenging everyday forms of racism, but to work with grassroots and local teams in order to begin conversations about racism and antiracism. This is also evident at a broader level in the efforts to use the Taking the Knee initiative in popular American sports such as the NFL and NBA to address both historical and contemporary issues about race. Initiatives such as these have helped to highlight the ways in which issues about racial injustice are part of popular sport culture as well as of the wider society (Dixon, Cashmore and Cleland 2022; Houghteling and Dantzler 2020). But they have also helped to highlight the potential role of popular sport, whether at the professional or the grassroots level, as a means of challenging racism in everyday contexts as well as institutionally.

Forming alliances, making change

Another important aspect of antiracism has been the question of how best to form alliances, both politically and in civil society, in order to facilitate change and overcome resistance. This has been a feature of antiracist mobilizations and movements both historically and in the present. A recurrent theme in debates on the development of minority political action is the question of political alliances between black and ethnic minority and antiracist political groups. The need for such alliances is based on two assumptions. First, it is argued that the relatively small size of the minority population means that their demands would have a greater chance of success if they had the support of at least some sections of the majority white population. The second assumption is that racism is as much a problem for the white majority as it is for the ethnic minorities, and that racist political groups and movements can best be dealt with by an alliance between black and ethnic minority and antiracist groups. More generally, it is argued that antiracist mobilizations can help to create possibilities for alliances that address the ways in which processes of racialized exclusion shape the everyday experiences of race and racism in contemporary society.

The need for collective mobilizations across racialized boundaries lies at the heart of efforts to bring movements and actors from different backgrounds into antiracist interventions. From this perspective, George Lipsitz has argued that a characteristic of antiracist mobilizations lies in their efforts to bring together seemingly illogical forms of opposition:

Antiracist social movement organizations raising seemingly illogical forms of opposition, however, fight for processes of collective participation. They argue that houseless people who own little or no property have every right to inhabit the city and help determine its future. They recruit high school students to

write about the conditions they encounter in their everyday
lives, to participate in social movement mobilizations, to learn
how to find something left to love in themselves and in others
in their community in the midst of oppressive circumstances
that can make people unlovable. (Lipsitz 2019: 289)

The point Lipsitz is highlighting here is that mobilizations
can be seemingly illogical, and indeed focused on very specific
issues, and at the same time help to bring diverse groups of
people and interests together to address issues of common
concern, whether at national or local levels.

An example of efforts to form alliances that are framed
around a common commitment to antiracism can be found in
the ongoing mobilizations by feminist organizations over the
past few decades. Although there were many tensions around
questions of race and ethnicity within feminism through this
period, there have also been sustained examples of everyday
work to create alliances based on common interests and a
commitment to social justice. Part of the challenge faced in
these efforts to address antiracism in the context of feminist
mobilizations has been addressed by a range of scholars who
have focused on the intersections of race, gender and class as
sites of mobilization (Collins 2024; Crenshaw 2019b; Srivastava
2024). It is also of some significance that, although there have
been efforts to form alliances across feminist and antiracist
communities of interest, there have also been ongoing tensions about the practical workings of these efforts.

Over the past few decades, we have seen a meshing together
between antiracism and the ideas and values articulated within
black feminist scholars' organizations and alliances of activists
(Collins 2024; Hawthorne and Lewis 2023; Srivastava 2024).
This coalescence between black feminist activism and movements such as Black Lives Matter has been highlighted in
the research of a number of scholars. Marcia Chatelain, for
example, has noted that much of the analysis of the movement,

from both the right and the left, tends to not fully recognize the nuances and complexities of its relationship to black feminist sensibilities and values:

> Across the ideological spectrum, critiques of BLM have disregarded the nuances of black politics. The right vilifies black activism that challenges white supremacy for undermining national myths, including the idea that all change happens gradually. The left, meanwhile, which has fully embraced class analysis but still struggles to grasp the depths of anti-blackness, is often unable to understand black activism's many shapes and forms, including the black feminist principles that have been so central to the organizing of the last five years. (Chatelain 2019: 129)

The key point that Chatelain, and other scholars, have noted about Black Lives Matter is the influence of ideas about organizing for change that underpin much of the work of organizations that have helped to shape the movement and its development over the past decade. She also highlights the role that black feminist values have played in shaping both the ideological values of the movement and its struggles to bring together a broad alliance for change. But, in emphasizing black activism's many shapes and forms, she is also arguing that it is not a singular movement, but a collection of initiatives aimed at tackling racial and other forms of injustice.

It is also important to recognize that, in some contexts, antiracist mobilizations have sought to bring together communities of identity based on both race and religion. This has been highlighted by research that shows that some religious groups have mobilized successfully on questions linked to racial justice as well as migrants' rights. An important site for these mobilizations has been the question of the position of migrants and refugees who seek to enter the United States and Europe (Christerson, Salvatierra, Romero and Yuen 2023; Han and

Arora 2022). Such mobilizations have often been framed by both religious ideas of a common humanity and broader ideas about antiracism. But the very existence of such mobilizations symbolizes the ways in which some faith-based organizations have become part of movements that seek to challenge racism in the present, often involving interactions with activists from non-faith-based organizations. Such mobilizations are not in practice a majority voice in many faith-based communities, and in the United States in particular we have seen both white nationalist and racist ideas and values within sections of evangelical Christianity. Indeed, strident voices in support of white supremacy and extreme Christian nationalism have been a recognizable part of faith-based communities over the past few decades (Davis and Perry 2021; Yancy and Bywater 2024). But at the same time, it is important to recognize that faith-based communities have played, and continue to play, important roles on the ground in supporting antiracist forms of mobilization.

There are also signs that there has been increasing awareness and calls for reparations in relation to transatlantic slavery within religious institutions at a broader level. An example of such mobilizations can be found in the efforts within the Church of England to address its historical links, both economic and material, to transatlantic slavery. A report by the Church Commissioners for England found extensive evidence of the linkages between the official church and chattel slavery and recommended that the Church set up a fund to provide some remedy for its role in supporting and benefitting from slavery (Church Commissioners for England 2023). Although the report led to an extensive debate about both the amount of the fund set up for reparations and the substance of the Church's role in supporting slavery, it helped to highlight the complex ways in which the legacies of slavery and racism remain embedded in core religious, cultural and educational institutions. But it also drew attention to the work of those within the Church who were seeking both to come to terms with its history and to ensure that it played an active role in seeking to remedy the past and to tackle the legacies of racism in the present.

Much of the research and scholarship on Black Lives Matter has also highlighted the ongoing tensions about how best to gain access to resources and influence, whether through the mainstream or alternative political spheres (Johnson 2023; Ostertag 2019). For some, it is a movement that has a strong focus on protest and expressive politics and on developing alliances in favour of more radical social change. Alvin Tillery argues:

> For now, it is sufficient to say that, by judging all of this evidence in context, the SMOs examined in the study are building a movement that is focused much more on expressive communication than strategic communication aimed at mobilizing resources and negotiating directly with the elites who control the levers of power that are making African Americans vulnerable to police brutality and other forms of predation. (Tillery 2019: 319)

The key point being made here is that, in practice, the mobilizations surrounding Black Lives Matter are focused on gaining an audience for an agenda for social change in society and not on gaining some limited access to representative political institutions. In this sense, it can be seen as a movement that is political, but not as a movement that limits itself to the boundaries of mainstream political representation. Yet, for others, it is also important to locate such recent mobilizations against the longer background of struggles for racial justice that involved efforts to challenge the political, legal and economic structures that kept the dominant racial order of the United States in place (Dawson 2011; 2014; Dawson and Francis 2015; Reed Jr. 2016; 2018).

As was argued earlier on, the mobilizations around the Black Lives Matter movement have been at the heart of the push for radical changes in relation to the position of racialized minorities in contemporary societies. Part of the challenge represented by Black Lives Matter is that it is not always clear how – if at all – some of the demands it is making are possible within the current social and political order. This is a point that is made forcefully by Minkah Makalani in his exploration of the demands being made under the banner of Black Lives Matter:

> The politically unimaginable is precisely what a liberal black politics finds itself unable to grapple with in Ferguson. We might even say that there is no way for liberal black politics to incorporate a Ferguson. This is in large part because the activists of Ferguson seem to reject the parameters of black electoral politics, national black leaders, and even progressive venues of political discourse. As a decentralized movement led by black women that locates police violence within larger structures of the state, and poverty, it presents a challenge to formal black political practices that seek access and power within those very structures. The result is that BLM and Ferguson, whose demands are generally beyond possible within the current political order, are largely unintelligible to those outside its organizational practices and political discourses. (Makalani 2017: 547–8)

Makalani's critical analysis of the role of Black Lives Matter highlights a tension that is likely to remain at the heart of both current and future debates about how to move towards more radical changes in the social and political structures that help to maintain racialized inequalities – namely, how to balance the demands for formal representation in the political sphere with radical mobilizations that seek to challenge capitalist society more generally. But in pointing towards the need to think beyond the boundaries of the formal public sphere and to discuss the politically unimaginable, he is also highlighting an issue that needs to be analysed in more detail – namely, the question of how we can navigate the real tensions that arise in societies such as the United States and the United Kingdom when the hopes for change and reform come up against the hard realities that have limited the possibilities for radical changes in the structures of racialized inequality.

Limits and contradictions

In looking at the question of how antiracist policies and agendas have sought to move from theory to practice, it is important to explore the limits and contradictions of actually existing forms of antiracism. This is the focus of the concluding part of this chapter.

Part of the reason for the intensity of debates about actually existing antiracism is that there is an acknowledgement that there remains a significant gap between antiracist aspirations and the realities of limited and often contradictory outcomes of antiracist policies and initiatives across a wide range of policy arenas. This is evident in the bodies of research that have highlighted the continuing significance of race in helping to shape opportunities in key areas such as employment, housing, education and health (Andersen 2021; Finney et al. 2023). It is also clear from the ongoing conversations about racial inequalities that are very much part of the political culture of a large number of contemporary societies.

Yet, despite this gap, it can be argued that the impact of antiracism over the past few decades helped to institutionalize policies and practices that played a part in challenging racism at various levels. In his overview of the experiences of antiracism during the twentieth century, Alastair Bonnett argued that it can be seen as one of the key strategies that helped to facilitate change in the structural as well as the cultural forms of racism:

> Anti-racism has been one of the central liberatory currents of the twentieth century. It may be located in the struggle against European colonialism, and in the attempt to form multiracial, multicultural, international and national forms of governance. It can be seen at work in the development of forms of education and training that facilitate tolerant and cosmopolitan attitudes, as well as within everyday culture. (Bonnett 2000)

Although Bonnett's overview was written at a time when there was perhaps a more positive policy climate in relation to efforts to tackle racism and promote changes in everyday attitudes about race and culture, it can be argued that he helpfully captures the range of political and social practices that were shaped by forms of antiracist thinking over the long twentieth century.

In the contemporary context, the attitude to antiracism is in many ways less positive, and there have also been a number of critical voices in relation to the impact of antiracism. Kenan Malik, for example, has argued that in the present context a key trend in antiracist politics has been an emphasis on symbolic identity politics and representational fairness rather than on efforts to challenge structural social and political inequalities (Malik 2023). Malik's point of critique is aimed at the limitations of what he sees as a traditional left politics of race, which he sees as tied up with a politics of identity that can also have negative consequences. Although he is not totally dismissive of antiracism, his emphasis is much more on what he sees as contradictions of antiracism as a form of identity politics.

What these arguments highlight is that there is a need to reframe analysis in such a way that we stop thinking of antiracism from the top and look at the ways we can begin to bring about changes at the level of the everyday and the local. In the period since the early 2000s, however, the question of how to develop strategies against racism has taken on new forms. This is partly because of the changing nature of racism itself. But it is also because it is during this period that we have seen a flowering of political discourses which proclaim antiracism as one of their key objectives. Within both academic and popular political debates, the issue of antiracism has come to occupy centre stage in much of the discussion in this field. But there is by no means agreement on how to develop a politics of antiracism in the present environment. The conceptual and ideological confusion we have highlighted above has seeped through into the debate about how to develop practical political strategies against racism. Above all, the very notion of antiracism has become an essentially contested one and there are divergent accounts of what is meant by it.

This is partly because of the lack of clarity as to what a politics of antiracism may mean in practice. In this environment, it is important to discuss more fully what a politics of antiracism may mean in the present. A starting point would be to move away from seeing antiracism as a catch-all term and to explore how it can be used to help make sense of diverse measures against racism and discrimination that can lead to practical initiatives to challenge racist practices. From this perspective, antiracism needs to be seen in essentially practical political terms, but also as necessarily entangled with the effort to tackle everyday forms of racism. Efforts to tackle racism and racial exclusion need to be seen as often involving multiple objectives, ranging from the whole society to initiatives targeted at specific everyday issues.

Within the terms of this account, there are two constituent elements of an antiracist politics. First, opposition to racist exclusion, ideologies and policies. Second, it needs to involve the articulation of new ways of recognizing and living with racial, ethnic and cultural difference. Such a strategy remains to some extent very focused and aimed at achieving strategic objectives, but it does highlight the need for political debates about racism to come to terms with wider debates about difference and the consequences of developing conceptions of justice and equality which allow for living together with difference while at the same tackling contemporary forms of racialized inequality.

While this account is by no means complete, it has the merit of situating perhaps the key dilemma which an antiracist politics has to confront in the present – namely, how to go beyond an essentially oppositional political stance to the articulation of an alternative view of racial and cultural difference to those to be found in racist discourses. While it is important to develop ongoing research and policy conversations about the workings of antiracism in practice, we have argued that it is equally essential to learn from the achievements of policies and interventions that have helped to shape many societies through the second half of the twentieth century and the first few decades of the twenty-first. It is important to acknowledge the limits of what has been achieved thus far, but there are also dangers in arguing that there has been no impact from the antiracist policies and interventions that have been pursued over the past few decades in Europe, North America, Brazil and other societies.

This is not to say that the idea of developing antiracist practices – whether at a broad social level or within specific governmental, public and private institutions – can be easily achieved, given the everyday realities of racialized inequalities that have been shaped both by the legacies of the past and the everyday processes that continue to shape forms of racial injustice and inequalities in the contemporary environment.

It should be evident from what we have seen thus far that there is a clear need to begin to think differently about what antiracism may mean today, rather than what it meant at the end of the twentieth century. In the contemporary environment, the political debates about populism, white nationalism and the politics of racism require a political and social response that can address the kinds of racial politics and mobilizations that have come to the fore in this first part of the twenty-first century (Bojadžijev 2020). This requires, more importantly, the development of an antiracist imaginary that can begin to develop initiatives at different scales to tackle contemporary racisms, both in the context of everyday social relations and interactions and in the context of the political sphere.

While it is important to develop a rounded analysis of the limits and contradictions of antiracisms in practice, it is also necessary to look at the possibilities for challenging racism through both policy interventions at societal level and the actions of individuals and movements.

4

One Step Forwards, Two Steps Back

Against the background of the key themes that we have discussed in chapters 1 to 3, we have emphasized the need to see antiracism as involving a complex set of ideological and political influences, rather than seeing it as a singular phenomenon. Indeed, we have argued that, just as a number of scholars have pointed us in the direction of seeing *racisms* in the plural, both historically and in the present, it is important that we see *antiracisms* as shaped by a wide range of ideological values, strategies for change and types of mobilization. Rather than searching for a singular form of antiracism to tackle the question of imagining and building strategies that aim to end the social, economic and political impact of racism, we need to envision ways of bringing about racial justice through a variety of approaches. More importantly, we also need to avoid the temptation to focus on the limits of antiracism in practice, however real they may be, and to explore ways in which we can develop conversations about what kinds of strategies for change may prove to be more effective going forwards. This is not to deny the relevance of a degree of pessimism about what has been achieved in the various efforts to tackle the continuing role of racism in our societies. Indeed, there may well be much we can learn from a critical engagement with the relative failures of policies and strategies aimed at tackling racism from the second half of the twentieth century to the present. But it is also important to be able to look for some hope and evidence of change among the ruins of past strategies and agendas for reform and progress.

This becomes even more evident if we shift our focus from the environment of academic and scholarly research on antiracism and look more broadly at the ongoing political and policy conversations, and everyday mobilizations at different local and national scales, around how we can develop strategies in practice that seek to tackle the structural and individual forms of racism in contemporary societies. It is with this in mind that we move on in this chapter to explore the question of what kinds of difference antiracism has made or failed to make in tackling the key forms of racism and racial division in the world around us. In particular, we shall focus on questions about the impact of antiracist policies and strategies on the world around us, at a time when we have seen increasing critiques from both the left and right of the political spectrum about the efficacy of antiracism as a mechanism for challenging racial inequalities and racist ideologies.

What kind of difference has antiracism made?

As the title of this chapter suggests, I shall also be arguing that there is a need to move away from seeing progress towards racial equality and justice as linear, in the sense that a move towards some kind of antiracist future is inevitable. Rather, as I have suggested already, it is likely that any kind of change is likely to be uneven and become a site for contestation and opposition from some sections of society and political interests. Indeed, as has become evident over the past two decades, antiracism has become one of the sites of the so-called 'culture wars' that have become part of the political culture of a broad range of societies. In this environment, part of the everyday reality we face in the world around us is how to create support for policies and initiatives that seek to eliminate racism as a substantive social phenomenon.

At the same time, we have suggested that there are dangers in seeing antiracism as inevitably failing, short of a radical anti-capitalist transformation or revolutionary change. This is the brunt of some of the most notable critiques of antiracism from the left, which seek to highlight the relative failure to move towards a post-capitalist future (Kundnani 2023; Shafi and Nagdee 2022). Such arguments can be seen as helping to highlight the need for more radical agendas in terms of policy and political priorities, and in this sense they are contributing to a critical analysis of the limits of actually existing antiracism. But the assumptions on which they are based are not helpful in making sense of the complexities of struggles for racial equality and justice in the present. Rather, I argue that it is important to hold on to the idea that struggles against racism and for racial justice can succeed in the world around us, even if progress is often uneven or involves efforts to push back against the reforms and changes that have been achieved in earlier periods of struggle and mobilization.

A key challenge that we need to address more fully is the reality that there is clear evidence over the past few decades that policies and interventions aimed at tackling racialized inequalities often involve a messy and complex pattern of some positive changes as well as some steps backwards. Rather than seeing antiracism as a uniform set of ideas and practices, it is important to envision it as often involving some positive achievements, but often bounded by limits and contradictions in terms of the broader goal of moving towards the elimination of racism. While we shall explore the limitations of what has been achieved in terms of change over the past few decades, we shall also argue that it is important to pay attention to the ways in which antiracist policies and practices have become embedded in specific environments and the possibilities for more radical initiatives in the future. This means developing an analytical framework that can allow us to empirically explore the role of antiracism in specific places, institutions and environments.

In this context, it is important to address the question of what difference antiracism has made at a practical level in tackling the changing forms of racism and racialized inequalities in contemporary societies. In the current political climate, it is important to develop an open conversation about the possibilities for antiracist policy initiatives to lead to changes in the institutional and structural expressions of racism in the world around us. In much of the scholarship in this field, there has been an unfortunate tendency to neglect the possibilities for antiracism and resistance by focusing on the structures and institutions that have helped to entrench racialized inequalities in contemporary societies. Whatever the reasons for this emphasis in research agendas, this has resulted in relatively little research on processes of resistance to racism. From this perspective, it is important to question both the taken-for-granted assumption that resistance to the structures of racism has lacked impact and the assumption that, given the nature of inequality and injustice more generally in our societies, antiracist initiatives are likely to fail or at least not make a substantial impact.

This neglect of forms of resistance to racism has been remedied to some extent by emerging research agendas that have placed much more emphasis on analysing the formation of antiracist movements, the role of resistance by racialized minorities and the creation of an antiracist imaginary. But it remains important to develop fuller research agendas in this area that can help to give voice to hidden histories of resistance in different historical conjunctures, as well as uncovering the role of agency in resisting racialized exclusion and domination.

Given the challenges we face in developing both theoretical and empirical research in the broad fields covered in this
volume, it is important that we begin a conversation about
what theoretical and empirical tools we need to help us to both
make sense of current trends and developments and begin
to contribute to discussions about which policy and political
interventions can help to tackle the root causes of racism and
forms of racial exclusion. It is also important for scholars and
researchers working on questions about race, racism and ethnicity to look beyond their own national contexts and engage
in open conversations with the concepts and analytical frames
that have emerged over the past few decades in different parts
of the globe.

There is nothing wrong as such in developing theoretical
and empirical research agendas that are framed by specific
histories, trajectories, histories of colonialism and migration,
and indeed it is inevitable that this will happen. But what is
less productive is a tendency to discuss the theoretical frames
and models developed in one national context as though they
are the only way to think through the complex ways in which
race and ethnicity shape the social world around us on a global
scale, with little or no acknowledgement of the work going on
in diverse academic communities across the globe. This is most
obvious in accounts of racism and antiracism that assume in a
taken-for-granted manner that the analytical frames developed
in the US are applicable to the rest of the world, with little or no
acknowledgement of different histories and political cultures.
This is an assumption that needs to be challenged, and we have
seen efforts to question it and develop more of a comparative analytical frame. It is also necessary to make the question
about possible routes to change part of the conversation in
critical scholarship about the dilemmas we face in dealing with
racial and ethnic difference in the world around us.

Antiracism and power relations

Although it is important to focus on the structural processes that have helped to entrench racialized inequalities, it is also necessary to keep a focus on avenues for change that are either possible in the present environment or likely in the future. As a number of scholars have suggested, it is precisely at times of uncertainty that we need to hold on to the hope that reforms and changes are possible (Back 2021; Cobb 2020; Glaude 2020; Mbembe 2017; Walcott 2021). In the present environment, it remains important to keep in perspective possibilities of hope, at a time when there seems to be little possibility for radical change and transformation in the ongoing efforts to address the racial inequalities and divisions that have been part of our histories over a number of centuries and which continue to shape the world around us today.

The possibility of hope is a key theme that has been taken up by Paul Gilroy in his critical reflections on the masses of humanity who have sought to reach Europe by crossing the Mediterranean, often at the risk of death. Reflecting on the realities of these crossings, Gilroy has sought to salvage the possibility of hope in the contemporary conjuncture, despite the reality that many of the human beings attempting the crossing to Europe are likely to lose their lives:

> I want to suggest that our responsibility to ourselves and to the people in the water, now and in the future, must show how, against the effects of what Fanon called epidermalisation, something like a 'real dialectic between the body and the world' can be reasserted. Perhaps it has already begun, unanticipated, to appear in the politics of sympathy discernible in the shadows of disaster. I hope you will be prepared to join with or at least endorse that ongoing, collective work of salvage. It is likely to involve more than pulling imperilled fellow beings from the sea, for it is our own humanity that needs to be rescued from

the mounting wreckage. There is still time for that operation, but not much. (Gilroy 2019)

It is important to remember that Gilroy's reference to 'pulling imperilled fellow beings from the sea' was written at a time when many migrants and refugees were dying in the Mediterranean and the Aegean seas in their search for the relative safety of Europe. As we are finishing this book, more of our fellow human beings are losing their lives in their efforts to reach Britain by crossing in small boats from France across the English Channel. Gilroy's call for rescuing *our own humanity* is a familiar theme in his influential body of scholarship over the past few decades (Gilroy 2018; Gilroy, Sandset, Bangstad and Høibjerg 2018), although it sometimes feels that such calls have not been well received in broader bodies of scholarly research into racism and antiracism, since these operate with a much more fixed notion of what can be done to develop a politics that addresses the root causes of racial inequalities and divisions.

Nevertheless, the call for a 'collective work of salvage' is an important point of reference here since it helpfully highlights the importance of developing conversations and research agendas about where we can find a politics of hope in and through the everyday realities of racial and ethnic division in the world around us, and the very real struggles of our fellow human beings to reach places of safety in times of insecurity. In addressing these issues, we need to look at how we can develop a broader account of antiracism that can allow us to explore power relations and policy agendas in a critical manner.

At the heart of the struggles around antiracism, there remain important questions about politics and power relations that will help to shape the future of efforts to move beyond racial categorization and its associated inequalities. Differential access to power is an important facet of the histories of racism over the past few centuries, and although we have seen important transformations in these power relations over the recent decades, they remain an important element of efforts to work towards the elimination of racism in contemporary societies.

In recognition of the uneven nature of power relations in the context of antiracism, some scholars have called for a more *reflexive antiracism* that starts off from the premise that both racisms and antiracisms are inextricably caught up in power relations. A good example of this approach can be found in the research of Kowal, Franklin and Paradies on diversity training (Kowal, Franklin and Paradies 2013). Drawing on their extensive research experiences in this field, they argue that a more reflexive antiracism is necessary in order to address questions of power relations and how they are shaped by both racism and antiracism:

> Reflexive antiracism allows antiracists to recognise that, within a racialised field, the division between racism and antiracism is often unclear and in flux. As white people working in a racialised field where members of minority groups routinely experience race oppression, they are perpetually susceptible to accusations of racism, either by other white antiracists or by members of minority groups. Consequently, they need to be secure enough in their identity to respond reflexively in such situations. Reflexive antiracism is therefore characterised by a reflexive stance towards one's own and others' attitudes, beliefs and behaviours while striving towards both equanimity in emotional reactions and a positive white identity. A reflexive antiracist approach encourages reflection on, and ultimately acceptance of, these tensions. (Kowal, Franklin and Paradies 2013: 326)

From this perspective, it is important both for antiracism to be seen as shaped by the complex histories of racism and for us to acknowledge that in the context of struggles against racism there will be inevitable tensions and conflicts. In this sense, it is not helpful to see antiracist activism or activists as speaking with one voice, when in practice there are always tensions around how best to address racism and how best to put anti-racist initiatives into practice. Though the key point made here is about the everyday experiences of white antiracist activists, the importance of the conceptual point made about *reflexive antiracism* can be seen as having a broader reach and is worth bearing in mind in thinking about broader histories of resistance and opposition to racism. This becomes even more evident if we look at the role that antiracist activists play in challenging specific forms of racial inequalities and injustice. It is to this issue that we now turn.

Activism and routes to change

In addressing the question of power relations, it is also important to include in any discussion of antiracism the role of antiracist activists in helping to develop mobilizations and organizations that seek to raise awareness and to take action to address specific types of racial injustice. Over the past few decades, activists have played an important role in helping to shape agendas in this field at all levels, and this is evident in the growing bodies of research that explores the range of activists in this field and their motivations and values (Ferguson 2023; Gorski 2018a). Some research has sought to explore more fully the motivations of both white antiracist activists and activists of colour, although this remains an area where we need more grounded research on specific movements and mobilizations in order to better comprehend the range of processes that help to motivate activists and shape their actions and praxis.

But, on the basis of existing research, it is evident that anti-racist activists have also become an important source of efforts to create and re-create forms of solidarity and support with victims of racism. An example of this process can be found in the ways in which activists have sought to use slogans such as 'City of Sanctuary' to address questions about racial injustice and exclusion in a diverse range of settings (Darling and Bauder 2019). The idea behind these mobilizations is both to assert the importance of providing spaces for caring for marginalized others who are seen as in need of support and assistance, and to symbolically highlight the idea that we are all part of the same humanity (Benhabib 2004). Such interventions have taken a wide range of forms over recent years, including efforts to encourage cities, local authorities, religious institutions and universities to set up programmes that involve support and care for undocumented migrants, refugees and others who are in need at particular points in time (Georgiou, Hall and Dajani 2022; Humphris 2023; Keskinen, Alemanji and Seikkula 2024). Although these efforts to symbolically use the idea of *sanctuary* to signal solidarity and care for fellow human beings who are vulnerable have taken a variety of forms, they have been premised on values that have been popularized by the trends and developments that we have outlined above.

An important facet of key developments in antiracist mobilization over the past two decades has been the formation of a diverse range of activists who have become the backbone of the various local, national and transnational developments in this period. What is even more important to note is that these activists have often taken a variety of routes towards being involved in antiracism, and it is not really possible to see them as being part of one collective antiracist identity as such. Much of their motivation may come from a broad commitment to challenge forms of racism and exclusion, but it is also evident from research over the past decade that they are also likely to be motivated by particular local issues or even by efforts to support and care for vulnerable individuals or families in need. It is clear too that activists are often drawn together from a wide range of racial and ethnic backgrounds, and that they bring with them diverse interests and concerns.

At the same time, it is important to note that research on the evolution of various forms of antiracist activism has highlighted that a core part of the activists are often from white majority backgrounds, often from a very diverse range of situations and with different political and social values. Their routes to engagement and involvement with antiracist mobilizations and movements have attracted much attention in recent years. Research that has explored their motivations for getting involved with antiracism has emphasized that the impetus for them to take part in various forms of direct or indirect activism is often shaped by experiences in education, in faith communities and in local and community groups, and more broadly by popular culture.

Although we have seen important insights into the background and motivations of those who become involved with – or at least are sympathetic to – antiracist activism, there is a need for more detailed accounts of the role and impact of such mobilizations. Such research is important if we are going to be able to develop a better understanding of the avenues for change in the contemporary environment.

Antiracism and popular culture

Another arena in which modes of activism and antiracism have come to the fore in recent times can be found in various fields of popular culture, including literature, cinema, music and popular sport. As we have already noted, efforts to use popular culture in the name of antiracism are not in themselves new, but there has been a proliferation of these efforts over the past two decades or so.

It is also important that, in thinking about antiracisms in the present, we do not just focus on politics and policy in the narrow sense. As was argued earlier, antiracist values and ideas have been expressed through a number of everyday forms of resistance to racism, including music, sport, art, and literature and poetry. These forms of everyday – and sometimes taken-for-granted – antiracisms have played an important role over the past few decades but they are often not addressed in the main bodies of research or scholarship in this field. Yet, in many ways, it remains important to broaden our vision of what kinds of antiracist voices we need by including popular culture in our analytical frames. Even a quick glance at the work of key black and minority writers, poets and public intellectuals – such as Zora Neale Hurston, James Baldwin, Toni Morrison and Maya Angelou – brings to light the way their work helped to address questions about racism and racial injustice. The same point can be made in relation to other key areas of popular culture over the past few decades, including sport and music. One particular poem by Maya Angelou comes to mind in this context – namely, her poem 'Still I Rise'. Angelou used this terse poem to capture an important feature of the values of fighting racism through her own life story and everyday experiences. She writes:

> You may write me down in history
> With your bitter, twisted lies,
> You may trod me in the very dirt
> But still, like dust, I'll rise
>   (Angelou 1986: 45)

A key point being made by Angelou in this poem, and in her work more generally, is that, whatever the trials and tribulations of racism and the erasure of race and racism from history, it is not really possible to silence her or others. Writers and commentators such as Angelou have played a significant and continuing role in developing public knowledge and understanding about the impact and legacies of racism, and it is important to include their voices as fully as possible in any rounded analysis of how we may be able to move beyond both racism and antiracism.

Another key arena in which questions about racism and antiracism have been played out in recent years has been in professional sport. A particular example of the complexities of the often taken-for-granted connections between the nation and racialized identities can be found in the ways in which questions about racism and antiracism have become entangled in the context of football in British society over the past few decades. There is a much longer history of the entanglements between race and racism in the context of football, particularly in the moral panics about racism and hooligan football cultures during the 1970s and 1980s (Back, Crabbe and Solomos 2001). But in the period since the 1990s, we have seen sustained efforts by antiracist activists to challenge the popular association of sections of the football fanbase of many professional clubs with racism, leading to the launch of the campaign organization Kick it Out, and widespread efforts by individual clubs and supporters' organizations to give voice to oppositional stances. There continues to be a lively debate about the impact of these mobilizations, with some researchers and commentators questioning their effectiveness, but in many ways the past three decades or so have provided at least some evidence that both governing bodies and individual football clubs are seeking to use the popular cultural capital associated with football culture to challenge expressions of racism, on the terraces at least (Kassimeris, Lawrence and Pipini 2022; Kick it Out 2023; Penfold and Cleland 2022). There is perhaps rather less evidence that the efforts to transform the boardrooms of clubs and the representational bodies of the sport have had much impact, but the overall story of the past few decades has at least seen some substantial efforts to address racism among supporters.

The extent of the impact of initiatives such as Kick It Out remains a contested issue, however, particularly when examples of racism come to the fore in relation to specific events. In 2021, for example, during the UEFA Euro 2020 tournament, a number of events led to intense debate about the limits of the changes that had been brought about by various antiracist initiatives over the previous three decades. England's national football team reached the final of the tournament with a team composed of a racially and ethnically diverse group of players and, in the run-up to the final, there was an ongoing conversation on both social media and the national press, radio and television about the team and what it symbolized regarding the role of diversity and difference in British society. In the end, England lost the final to Italy on penalties. Three of the players who missed penalties for England were Bukayo Saka, Jadon Sancho and Marcus Rashford. In the aftermath of the game, all three players were the subject of racial abuse, particularly on social media. It should be noted that, in the months that followed, there ensued an often angst-riven conversation about what the abuse directed at Saka, Sancho and Rashford symbolized about questions of race and national identity (Back and Mills 2021; Penfold and Cleland 2022; Szatan 2021). Much of this discussion contained expressions of support for the three players, and shock at the turn of events that led to the outpouring of racial abuse directed at the three young footballers.

But what this event has helpfully highlighted is that, even at a time when the England national football team is invoked as a symbol of diversity and as representing a kind of national togetherness, the imagined community of who belongs to the nation remains fragile and contested. The events in the aftermath of the Euro20 final have been interpreted from a variety of perspectives. For some, they highlight the ways in which, despite popular celebrations of diversity and multiculturalism, and ongoing efforts by organizations such as Kick It Out to address questions about expressions of racism among supporters as well as in the institutions of the sport, there remain important ways in which racism remains embedded among sections of fans. For others, they highlight the ways in which, despite the efforts by racists and others to question the inclusion of black players into the national imaginary, there are also clear signs that for many supporters they have in fact become part of the imagined national community.

Corporate antiracism

It has also become evident over the past few decades that we have seen the emergence and impact of forms of corporate antiracism and multiculturalism. Although this phenomenon attracted attention in the context of corporate responses to the mobilizations around Black Lives Matter, it can best be seen as part of an ongoing process involving key actors in the private corporate sector that has a longer historical presence. Indeed, even at the end of the twentieth century and in the early 2000s, there were signs that global corporations were becoming engaged with issues linked to multiculturalism, antiracism and diversity more generally. What has perhaps helped to attract more attention to this phenomenon over the past two decades is that we have seen more high-profile corporations declare themselves as committed to the idea of taking action to deal with racism and historical patterns of exclusion. But in the immediate aftermath of the protests surrounding the death of George Floyd in 2020, a large number of major American corporations issued statements that sought to signal their commitment to ideas of racial justice and equality, though avoiding the more radical and political statements linked to Black Lives Matter mobilizations more generally. This included global corporations such as Nike, Apple, Gap, Walt Disney and Walmart. For some scholars, these kinds of statements are seen as representing a type of *corporate #BLM speech*, often detached from any more controversial language about the history of racism and its contemporary forms (Fairfax 2022; George 2021; Ramirez 2023). Yet it is also clear that, although these corporations did not seek to engage with more radical strands of antiracist mobilizations, they did want to highlight their overarching commitment to opposing racism and discrimination, as well as their promotion of equal opportunity in hiring and promotion practices within their organizations (Elias, Ben and Hiruy 2023).

The reach and extent of corporate initiatives in this field has been much debated in recent years. Indeed, in the aftermath of the public debates about Black Lives Matter over the past decade or so, there was something of a concern among some activists that large corporations were almost adopting the language of the movement and even its imagery and symbols in order to incorporate it through what some scholars see as a kind of *neoliberal antiracism* (Fairfax 2022; Nelson and Dunn 2017). But, whatever the motivations for these corporate involvements with antiracism, it seems clear that a number of key global corporations have a degree of motivation for getting involved with these issues. It is also important, of course, to note that a number of corporations have pointedly not expressed any form of support for mobilizations against racism and have largely remained silent when faced with pressure to do so.

It is evident as well in the strategies and policies adopted in professional contexts in the private sector, such as corporate legal and finance firms, over the same period, as they seek to engage with issues around diversity, including race, gender and sexuality. Whatever the merits of such initiatives in terms of their impact, it is important to address questions about racial equality and diversity in such sectors, since in practice imagining that such issues are not of concern to the professional sector is not really a tenable position, given all the trends and developments that we have seen in recent times. Indeed, pressures to address questions of exclusion and diversity in sectors such as the legal profession and higher education have come to the fore even more during the past decade.

The impact of such corporate and professional initiatives has been mixed in many sectors. As the mobilizations that took place under the banner of Black Lives Matter during 2020 have highlighted, the reality is that there continue to be deep divisions about the salience of race in shaping contemporary British society. At one level, the mobilizations led many institutions and large corporations to declare their symbolic commitment to racial equality and justice. In the field of sport, for example, football players in the Premier League 'took the knee' before the start of games throughout much of 2020, and added statements about Black Lives Matter and No Room for Racism to their shirts. These gestures generated their own racist responses to targeted black footballers. At the same time, all members of the Premier League have signed up to a commitment to bring about greater diversity at all levels of their organizational structure.

There have been a number of critiques of the incorporation of antiracism into the public discourses of mainstream institutions and large corporations (Blake, Ioanide and Reed 2019). The starting point of these critiques is the notion that the process of incorporation leads to a depoliticization of understandings of both racism and antiracism. There are also concerns expressed that much of the motivation for corporations' involvement with questions of race comes from commercial motives, and indeed can be seen as a form of window-dressing rather than a substantive commitment to tacking the broader structures of racism in society. While it is important to engage with these critiques of corporate antiracism, it is also necessary to explore whether the involvement of corporations and professional bodies is central to the development of antiracism in the future. Given their importance in the wider context of contemporary societies, it is necessary to develop strategies for change that include them as part of programmes for tackling institutional patterns of exclusion and discrimination.

The politics of anti-antiracism

One of the key developments we have seen over the past two decades or so has been the growth of critiques of antiracism from the right of the political spectrum. Such critiques are varied both in substance and in tone, but at a basic level they are held together by a set of ideas that can be seen as representing an anti-antiracist set of political values and ideas. It is in this evolving environment that we have seen a rapid expansion of efforts by both academic and public commentators to articulate critiques of antiracism from the right of the political spectrum.

It is perhaps not surprising in the current political climate that antiracism has become a deeply contested issue, with critics from both the right and left of the political spectrum focusing their critical glare on what they see as the limitations of antiracism, both from an ideological and from a practical perspective. It is also important to note in this context that it is partly because of the advances that have been made over the past few decades that we have seen a noticeable backlash against antiracism from sections of the conservative right and from sections of the liberal left who have become increasingly worried by migration and growing forms of racial, ethnic and religious diversity.

In some ways, this in itself is not a new phenomenon. For example, in his overview of antiracism in the 1980s and 1990s, Alastair Bonnett noted what he termed an 'anti-antiracism', partly in response to the emergence of antiracist social and political mobilizations over the same period. Bonnett noted at the time what he termed anti-antiracism was both a social and a political phenomenon, often shaped by the interventions of politicians and new right activists who sought to undermine the ideological basis or the need for antiracism. Although Bonnett's focus was more on the situation in the UK, he also noted that there were similar ideological and political trends in the US and more generally (Bonnett 2000). Key features of this backlash included an emphasis on seeing the growth of antiracism in areas such as education and in universities as a potential threat to cultural cohesion and national identity. Although this backlash was perhaps not on the same scale as the culture wars that have come to the fore over the past two decades, it can be seen in many ways as a kind of precursor to them, at least in the sense that it sought to argue that the real danger to social cohesion was not to be found in racism but in the efforts of antiracists to construct an ideology that sought to undermine Western values and civilization (Lewis 1988; Palmer 1986).

Since the early 2000s, however, we have seen a new form of this backlash, often framed in the language of the new right or neo-conservatism. This backlash has been more noticeable from thinkers from the right of the political spectrum, although it is also the case that some commentators who see themselves as on the liberal or left wing of political culture have also expressed various degrees of scepticism about the role that antiracism can play in challenging racial injustice in contemporary societies.

At the same time, however, we have seen a renewed emphasis on the need for counter-narratives to antiracism, particularly those that emphasize a traditional view of national identity based on shared values. This is evident in the interventions of new right and conservative commentators in the US, the UK and other national contexts over the past two decades as we have seen how various versions of culture wars about race and related issues become part of both academic and public discourses about race, as well as other forms of religious and cultural diversity.

This is evident in the critiques of public commentators such as David Goodhart, who self-identify as part of a liberal critique of antiracism and multiculturalism (Goodhart 2013; 2017). But it is also a clear part of the critiques of academics such as Matthew Goodwin and Eric Kaufmann, who see themselves as part of the neo-conservative critique of antiracism, and who voice a strident opposition not just to immigration, antidiscrimination policies and what they define as a liberal left political and cultural elite (Eatwell and Goodwin 2018; Goodwin 2023; Kaufmann 2017; 2018). Both Goodwin and Kaufmann see themselves as lone neo-conservative voices within an academic environment that they see as part of an elite culture that ignores the interests of the white majority in British society by advocating the interests of racial and other cultural minorities.

In this context, another voice from the ideologically conservative critique of antiracism can be found in the work of public commentators such as Douglas Murray (Murray 2017; 2019), who have been active in a number of neo-conservative think tanks over the past two decades. Murray has been a key figure in neo-conservative circles and has been voicing concerns about immigration, antiracist initiatives and the threats – as he sees them – presented to European and Western culture by radical Islam and other *enemies within*.

An increasing number of critiques of antiracism have been voiced by members of black and ethnic minority communities, particularly in the United States. Although such voices have been part of the landscape of public debates about race there for a number of decades, it is also clear that they have become much more strident and angry as the wider political climate around questions of race has become deeply fractured.

Critiques of antiracism have also become part of the debates about race outside of the US political landscape. An example of the broader reach of this approach can be found in the work of Rakib Ehsan, who has been influenced by the work of black conservative scholars in the US as well as by various think tanks based there, and has argued that what he calls grievance culture has become an integral part of what he sees as the race relations industry (Ehsan 2023). Ehsan's main targets are left and antiracist activists, whom he sees as ideologues of what he terms a *grievance culture* about race, which is not really interested in advancing the position of racial and ethnic minorities but, rather, motivated by their own ideological commitment to what he sees as an outdated politics of race.

A somewhat different take on these issues can be found in Tomiwa Owolade's effort to argue that the influence of radical American approaches to race has in effect distorted British discussions about racism and antiracism. Owolade positions himself as a public commentator and journalist who seeks to question dominant approaches to race in British society. In a book entitled *This Is Not America* (2023), Owolade has also sought to argue that, rather than mimicking the American discussions about race, we need to develop a more specifically British conversation about race. Although written in somewhat less strident tones than Ehsan's book, it is also essentially a critique not just of the influence of an overtly American take on race but also of what Owolade sees as an over-reliance on the importance of systemic and structural racism in accounts of the role of racism in British society.

Denials of racism

Perhaps the core theme to be found in the arguments framed by anti-antiracists is a denial of the social significance of racism. This is evident in the arguments of both new right and neo-conservative opponents of antiracism, who, as well as questioning the arguments developed by antiracists, often engage in denials of the importance of racism in the world around us. While not all commentators who articulate an anti-

antiracism perspective argue that racism does not exist as such, they nonetheless tend to see themselves as arguing against the ideological and political influence of antiracism, since they are frequently preoccupied by the need to defend what they see as the traditional values of the West against the efforts by anti-racists to suggest that there is a need for radical measures to tackle the legacies of racial domination and division.

A clear example of this process of denial can be found in the efforts of neo-conservative activists in the United States to question the need for radical measures to tackle racial inequalities. As the research of Rogers Smith and Desmond King has highlighted, American society can be seen today as deeply divided between activists who seek to repair past and present inequalities and those who oppose any such strategy in the name of protecting traditional American values and norms (Smith and King 2021; 2024). This is a deep-seated division and activists and thinkers opposed to any strategies of repair actively promote denials that racism is a substantive issue that needs to be addressed.

Although expressed in somewhat different political languages, we have seen similar types of political discourse being articulated more generally in Europe, Brazil and Australasia, for example. The arguments of scholars who identify themselves with versions of right-wing populism and the right have gone even further than those of commentators outside of the academy. An example of this strand of work can be found in the work of Frank Furedi in recent times. Although Furedi's intellectual trajectory has embraced a neo-Marxist cult in the past, he has now become publicly identified with key facets of new right and libertarian thinking, and he has voiced strong opposition to immigration and to race-focused social policies and interventions (Furedi 2018; 2021). In moving from a neo-Marxist cult to the politics of neo-conservative populism, Furedi has become a key intellectual influence behind an online magazine entitled *Spiked*, which openly mixes support for populism with strident opposition to any race-focused policies, and indeed any kind of politics focused on tackling systemic racism and discrimination in society. Although somewhat marginal in the context of mainstream politics, his views have been embraced by organizations linked to neo-conservative think tanks and activist groups.

We have also seen strong efforts by neo-conservative commentators in the United States to question the importance of racism in the context. Scholars such as Thomas Sowell have sought to undermine the arguments of both antiracist scholars and activists regarding the importance of racism (Sowell 1981; 2013). Sowell, in particular, has sought to question the underpinning arguments behind efforts to tackle racial inequalities, by outlining an ideological critique that questions the relevance of race as a social category and argues that it is largely an ideological construct of activists from the left rather than serving the interests of minorities as such.

The influence of these denials of the social significance of racism can also be traced in official government discourses that have sought in one way or another to shift the focus onto efforts to look for *racial and ethnic disparities* rather than racism as such. Efforts like this are not merely about the language that we use to talk about racial divisions and inequalities, since in talking about *racial disparities* there is also often an effort to avoid a substantive engagement with the question of racism per se, often accompanied by the rejection of measures to tackle institutional and systemic forms of racism in society. This is evident in the UK in the debates about the findings of the Commission on Race and Ethnic Disparities, which have been framed by government ministers as evidence of multi-faceted racial disparities, rather than as evidence of structural forms of racism in British society (Badenoch 2021; Commission on Race and Ethnic Disparities 2021; Minister of State for Equalities 2022). Such arguments are premised on a rejection of the wealth of empirical evidence pointing to the continuing significance of racism and racial inequalities, since this evidence is seen as produced by academics who are influenced by radical political agendas.

Taken together, these denials of the importance of racism and racial inequalities in contemporary societies represent perhaps what is still a marginal strand of both scholarly and public opinion, but there are also signs that these voices are growing louder in the present political environment. They have certainly become part of both academic and public intellectual debates in ways that have not been seen before, apart from in the American environment.

Ways forward

At the end of this chapter, it is important to return to the core underlying theme we have sought to outline – namely, that the impact of antiracism over the past few decades needs to be contextualized against the historical legacies of racial domination and exclusion and contemporary forms of racism that continue to structure social and political realities today. In making this point, the key underlying concern has been the need to explore the possibilities for a radical antiracist policy agenda to address both the complex forms of racial inequality and injustice in the present.

Part of the challenge we face in the contemporary environment is how to develop more open and critical conversations about antiracism that can take us beyond looking to the distant future for moving beyond the bounds of racism. It is important to be able to outline realistic strategies, backed up by policy and political interventions that offer the prospect of moving beyond racism in the present. In key areas of our societies, such as employment, education, health and the criminal justice system, there is a wealth of evidence that points to the everyday realities of racial division and exclusion.

Racisms and antiracisms are fashioned in interactively global and local circumstances, and it is increasingly difficult to separate out what is happening in particular geopolitical environments from broader global trends and conversations. A key point that we have sought to make in this chapter is that, by looking at contemporary forms of racism and antiracism as part of wider patterns of racialization, we can begin to make sense of the often messy and complex mechanisms that help to spread ideologies that reproduce racial categorization in the present.

Such commitments have been seen to some extent as symbolic, but they also help to highlight the gap that there remains between the promise of racial justice and equality and the continuing realities of enduring divisions and inequalities. A good example of the extent of this gap can be found in the report of the Joint Committee on Human Rights of the House of Commons and the House of Lords, which noted that 'The failings of successive governments to act in response to the successive reports and reviews shows that something is wrong with the architecture which is supposed to protect human rights and promote racial equality' (House of Commons 2020: 9).

In pointing out the seeming failure to move beyond promises to promote racial equality over an extended period, the Joint Committee also noted that the main government body responsible for initiating change in this field, namely the Equality and Human Rights Commission, had failed to provide leadership and direction at a time when there was a need to gain the trust of minority communities about the possibilities for effective action to remedy historically rooted inequalities.

It is important in the political climate that has developed around questions about race and racism globally over the past few decades to avoid the temptation to locate the possibilities for change around a singular and fixed version of antiracism. Rather, we need to be open to the possibility that we shall need a wide range of policy and political interventions in order both to advance racial justice specifically, and to tackle class and economic inequalities in our societies more generally. It is to these issues that we turn in the final chapter of this book.

5

Beyond Antiracism?

The arguments developed in this book thus far point to two key overarching themes. First is the need to centre antiracism in research, scholarly and public policy agendas. This means making every effort to develop our understandings of antiracism as an empirical object of research, rather than discussing it largely as a conceptual issue. Second, I have argued that it is important to work with the idea that there are in practice multiple antiracisms that need to be put into practice, depending on context and environment.

Both themes serve to highlight the need to take antiracism seriously in the evolving research agendas in this field, just as scholars involved in earlier conversations in the 1980s and 1990s sought to centre questions about racism in research and scholarly debates. As has been argued in different ways throughout the various chapters, this is going to be very much a process, and indeed there is growing evidence that awareness is already increasing among some scholars that this is a direction that we need to take if we are going to make scholarly research more directly relevant to efforts to tackle racism in the world, and to set in motion strategies for eliminating racism and its consequences. There is some way to go, but change is happening already.

We now move on to explore the implications of these core arguments for how we can begin to think beyond antiracism, particularly at a time when there remain major gaps in our understanding of the histories and the contemporary forms of antiracism. This is an important issue to address more fully, since in reality antiracism cannot be seen as an end in itself but as a series of strategies that aim to end the social and political significance of racism. While there is, rightly, a degree of scepticism about the oft-repeated claims over the past two decades that we have somehow transitioned into a kind of post-racial future, it is important to critically engage with the question of what a future beyond antiracism may actually look like and how we may be able to move towards it. This is why, in this concluding chapter, I want to take a look backwards by synthesizing the overarching themes developed in this book, as well as looking forwards by exploring how we can develop a fuller vision of what it means in practice for societies to move beyond racism. By covering both of these angles, we shall be able to address questions about the kinds of antiracist mobilizations and strategies that we need today in order to move towards the elimination of racism as a material force in our societies. As I will argue, it is also important in the current climate to engage with this question with a sense of creativity, humility, generosity and collaboration in order to carry out the detailed research and scholarship that is needed to be able to make a substantial contribution to challenging dominant research and policy agendas.

What kind of antiracism do we need today?

We have now reached the point in this book where we need to look more closely at an underlying theme that we have touched upon through its various components – namely, the issue of what it means today to look beyond racism and think about what kind of antiracist futures may become feasible. More prosaically, we need to explore the question of what kinds of antiracist strategies and agendas we need to address the real challenges we face in tackling the evolving and changing forms of racism that have come to the fore over the past few decades. As antiracism and racism are intertwined phenomena, it is important to address this connection from the very beginning.

A growing body of literature on racism mirrors central tensions, disagreement and different perspectives about how to analyse this phenomenon. Some scholars focus on the concept of racism; others, on xenophobia. Some see racism as a structural phenomenon intrinsic to societies, while others see it as a product of specific societal and historical circumstances. Particular variants of racism are also studied, and we see comparative approaches trying to grasp variations in racism – at times named 'racisms', to mark the plurality not only of origins and manifestations, but also of separate cores of racisms.

I have argued that it is time for scholars and researchers, as well as practitioners, to build on evolving research agendas to address the question of what kinds of antiracist initiatives we need, so that we can begin to envision radical initiatives to tackle the changing forms of racism that still shape the world around us. In developing these agendas, there is a need to initiate conversations between researchers and policy makers at all levels of society, whether it be in central and local government or in the private sector, in order to develop interventions that will lead to the radical changes in racism and racial inequality that have been demanded over the past few decades.

In addition, more attention needs to be given to the heterogeneity of antiracisms in the present. This includes the role of diverse identities and ideologies in the formation of antiracist discourses, practices and communities. Given the long and entrenched histories of racism and racialization in our societies, it is important to be open to diverse ideas and values in helping to create antiracist mobilizations, ranging across political, cultural and faith-based values.

It is on the basis of these two arguments that I have highlighted the urgent need to create and fashion intellectual spaces for scholars, politicians, activists and policy makers to reflect, critique their own practices and ideologies, and learn from experiences elsewhere. Some of the basis for these conversations can be found in the wealth of research-based and policy-focused evidence that highlights the persistence of racialized divisions and inequalities developing in our contemporary societies. Yet there remains an urgent need to develop collaborative and critical research agendas that address the question of possible antiracist futures in the context of the present.

Whether we look at North America or at the UK and other European societies, there are numerous studies that highlight a critical analysis of a future beyond racism, in terms of both its institutional and its ideological forms. This is why it remains important to address more fully the question of how we can move beyond the kinds of antiracist policies and interventions that have taken place over the past few decades. In developing this analysis, we shall see that we need to discuss the avenues for more radical reform and change that will address institutional and other forms of racism and provide a direction for living in diverse societies in the future.

It is also important to pay close attention to the evolving and ever changing ways in which the racisms we face today are quite different from the racial ideologies and values that were current in the past. There is an ongoing debate exploring to what extent it is possible to differentiate a racism based on biological characteristics and the hierarchy of races, and a racism based on a cultural paradigm and an ethnopluralist doctrine. While the biological racism of the past still lingers on, it is in general within narrow racist groupings at the margins of society. The current shift from biological race to culture, defined in terms of separated and autonomous groups, might paradoxically create the conditions for rearticulation of what a number of scholars have conceptualized as a *new racism*, in which essentialist notions of cultures legitimate racism (Balibar 2008; Balibar and Wallerstein 1991). In his classic account of the emergence of *new racism*, Martin Barker suggests that earlier forms of racism defined in terms of superiority and inferiority have shifted to a recent one, linked to a theory of human nature that claims it is normal to form a bounded community, where feelings of antagonism will inevitably be aroused if outsiders are admitted (Barker 1981). Although Barker was writing about trends that he witnessed in the 1970s, the key point he made about the role of new racisms remains one that we should pay close attention to in thinking about the kinds of antiracisms we need to nurture and develop in the contemporary environment.

It is also important that, in focusing on the present, we should still be open to the need to connect the current issues we face with the complex histories of racism and antiracism. An important contribution made by black radical feminists in this area can be found in their efforts to recover both the historical and contemporary traces of struggles by black women to claim justice and equality (Collins 2024; Nash 2019). This long history of struggles by black women has involved making issues of race and gender central to the efforts to insist that justice and equality remain to be achieved for many communities in the world around us.

Antiracist strategies and standpoints

An important facet of moving beyond the limitations of contemporary antiracism is the need to develop critical antiracist imaginaries that look beyond racism and begin to imagine how a society can move towards a lived reality that takes us beyond racialized divisions and exclusions. In the same way that races are socially and politically constructed, it is important to acknowledge that antiracism is not a fixed and unchanging set of ideas or values, but a set of standpoints that are made and remade through both everyday and policy conversations about the present and future of racism.

Given that antiracism is best seen not as a fixed ideology but as a set of ethical and political values that seek to highlight the importance of a commitment to equality, dignity and common humanity, what we need in the current environment is a clear agenda for how we can move forwards to address the racialized inequalities that continue to shape our societies. While it is important to be attentive to the historical and structural roots of contemporary racisms, it is also important to question a tendency in some forms of antiracist thinking to leave little room for change and reform in the societies that we are part of. Antiracist thinking needs to be able to speak directly to the evolving and changing forms of social and political struggles in the present, and not simply to focus on some idealized future beyond contemporary capitalist societies.

This is an approach that is also evident in the work of some critical scholars working on the changing dynamics of racism and antiracism in the present-day context. Daniel Martinez HoSang, whose work is focused on American society, articulates this approach when he posits:

> Yet what this analysis, and so many others like it, fails to recognize and engage is a political tradition of antiracism and racial justice that has forged, in the crucibles of racial domination and violence, demands for a world organized around new structures of power, possibility, and life – including possibilities of economic life beyond the demands of capitalism. Rather than seeking incorporation into dominant systems of power or a limited set of rights to participate in these systems, these

traditions of political imagination, cultural production, and collective struggle seek not only to challenge racial domination but also to reconstitute the society that has produced such a diminished view of humanity. (HoSang 2019: 74–5)

In making this point, HoSang is suggesting that we need to think more broadly about how we can help to transform both racial inequalities and divisions, but also other social divisions and inequalities in contemporary societies.

One example of the complexities of how antiracist struggles and political imaginaries are woven together can be found in Keisha Blain's scholarship on the histories of black feminist nationalism and its impact on struggles for racial justice and struggles for gender equality (Blain 2018; 2024). Drawing on the writings and experiences of black women as grassroots activists, as political leaders and as intellectuals, Blain provides an account of how the work of these diverse groups has often been at the heart of the struggles for racial justice, equality and democracy. She also suggests that, as we look to the future, it is important to pay close attention to these kinds of mobilizations in order to fully comprehend the possibilities for radical change in contemporary societies. In developing this analysis from a comparative frame, Blain is also suggesting that it is important to see the struggles of black women through a transnational lens.

Other scholars have suggested that part of the challenge we face in the contemporary environment is that, often, critical dialogues on such questions as antiracism, postcolonialism and decolonization have taken place in isolation, with little evident effort to learn from each other. Some scholars of indigenous communities, for example, have argued that there remains a need to decolonize the conceptualization of antiracism so that the experiences of indigeneity are not erased and silenced. This is the key point made by Bonita Lawrence and Enakshi Dua in their critical call for the decolonization of antiracism

(Lawrence and Dua 2005). This neglect of issues of indigeneity in discussions of antiracism, and indeed of racism, remains an issue that needs to be included more centrally in the conversations going on at the present time.

Reimagining a politics of racial justice

Another key challenge we face in the current environment is how to reimagine what kind of politics of racial justice we need today, given the difficulties that we face. It is crucial in the current conjuncture to reimagine a politics of racial justice that goes beyond the bounds of public policy per se, by refocusing attention both on state-centred initiatives against racism and racialized inequalities, and bottom up within communities and institutions that seek to outline a new vision of what a racially just society can look like. Nasar Meer has suggested that, in the contemporary environment, we have to develop a new language of racial justice, to address the challenges raised by the struggles that have come to the fore over the past two decades, rather than remaining constrained by the perspectives of the late twentieth century (Meer 2022; 2023). In particular, he suggests that we need to broaden our vision to take on board the changing forms of racialized inequalities that are shaping our current social and political environment.

The process of reimagining a broader and radical policy agenda needs to be part of a conversation that involves people working both in institutions and in movements to bring about change in the society as a whole (HoSang 2019; Santow 2023). From this perspective, it is also important to acknowledge that it is necessary to see the politics of racial justice as inextricably linked to the broader sets of inequalities in our societies. Indeed, as much of the recent scholarship on class, gender and other entrenched forms of social inequality has emphasized, it is important to see them as inextricably linked to each other

(Piketty 2014; Savage 2021). In focusing on the question of racial justice, it therefore inevitably means that it is crucial to address ongoing conversations about the possibilities of putting antiracism into practice in contemporary societies while at the same time being attentive to the need for policies that address related forms of inequality and exclusion, in order to develop policies that are inclusive of racialized inequalities but also go beyond them.

In addition, it is important to tackle head on the question of the political and policy choices that need to be made in the present in order to look forwards to a future where ideas about race and difference will have little or no social significance. Rejecting the power of racism means that we need to be attentive to both the detailed workings of racialized divisions in contemporary social and political relations and the possibilities of reimagining a politics of equity and social justice. As I have argued in this book, antiracism needs to be imagined more broadly than has been the practice over the past few decades. But it is equally important that we develop a critical empirical agenda that addresses the lessons we can learn from efforts to develop antiracist strategies and policies since the turn of the century.

A key feature of the range of issues that we have explored in this book is that the demands for change are not always based simply on questions about race and ethnicity, since they are also often linked to broader issues of social justice. Writing from a rather different perspective from some radical scholars, Charles Mills has developed the idea that an alternative political strategy to challenge the structures of racism in contemporary societies can be framed around the broad idea of a *black radical liberalism*. Mills offers this proposal because he argues that liberalism has failed to address the realities of racism and racial injustice both historically and in the present (Mills 2017). Drawing on his broader analysis of the racial contract, Mills argues that a *deracialized liberalism* is needed, which combines the objective of achieving racial justice with a larger social justice politics that brings together a concern to address the connections between racial, class and gender inequalities. Part of the difficulty, of course, is that the conditions for creating coalitions and alliances that can sustain a deracialized liberalism are not always obvious in many political environments, but the underlying arguments articulated by Mills and others remain an important challenge in the present political context.

It is also important to acknowledge here that a key component of any hope for radical change in relation to efforts to repair racism in the present has to engage more fully with what Terri Givens has defined as the lived experience of *radical empathy* (Givens 2021). In some ways, in developing this argument, Givens is highlighting the need to think across racial and other divided groups to create alliances for change that will benefit us all. But she is also suggesting that in the current climate a feeling of *radical empathy* helps not only to bridge divides but to allow for real change. She argues: 'Racial divides can cause us to see economic and societal benefits as a zero-sum game. Empathy allows us to see the humanity in others, and radical empathy moves us to work towards social justice and change that will benefit us all' (Givens 2021).

From this perspective, an important theme in the conversations we need to develop in the current environment needs to focus on promoting both a sense of *radical empathy* and developing the kinds of initiatives that can promote both social justice and racial justice. In addition, a key point that needs more research and reflection is the question of how everyday struggles for change can help to encourage a sense of radical empathy across divided societies and communities.

One example of the kinds of processes that Givens is referring to here can be found in the efforts to challenge the process of excluding mostly minority children from school and pushing them into the arms of the juvenile and criminal justice systems. In his investigation of what he terms the movement to dismantle the school-to-prison pipeline, Mark Warren has highlighted the often complex linkages between local and national mobilizations around this issue and the ways in which racial justice organizing often meshes with questions of class and gender (Warren 2021). Although not always framed through the language of antiracism, these mobilizations highlight a specific example of the range of concerns that can come together to address racial justice through social policy.

Another interesting example of the growing impact of contemporary discourses about empathy can be found in the engagement by universities with their own role in being shaped by the histories of slavery, colonialism and racism. Although much of the research and scholarship we have discussed in this book has been produced by those working in university institutions, it is only surprisingly recently that the gaze of these scholars and their institutions has been turned on these universities. In recent time, we have seen intense debate about the role of slavery and colonialism in shaping the histories of a number of universities in the United States, including Harvard, Brown and Duke (Harvard University, Presidential Committee on Harvard and the Legacy of Slavery 2022; Walters 2017). Much of the focus of this discussion has been on breaking the history of denial and silence about these linkages, but an important undercurrent has been focused on the question of the possible role of these very same institutions in developing strategies and policies that aim to tackle the legacies of racism in the present. There have also been a noticeable number of universities in Britain that have sought to come to terms with their own messy and often intimate connections to slavery and colonialism. This is a trend that has come to the fore in the context of ongoing conversations about slavery and its legacies, but also about Black Lives Matter, antiracism and efforts to decolonize the curriculum. Over the past decade or so, universities such as Cambridge, Bristol and Glasgow have produced reports that reflect on their involvements with slavery and its legacies (Mullen and Newman 2018; University of Bristol 2022; University of Cambridge 2022). A number of these institutions have also sought to set up initiatives that aim to use reparations as a way to help overcome the legacies of their connections to slavery, and to address contemporary forms of racism and inequalities based on race (Virdee, Taylor and Masterton 2021). Such initiatives by key universities remain relatively small scale in terms of the economic resources put into them, given the long historical processes that have shaped universities and other institutions. But they also serve to highlight the changes that may be possible if key institutions develop a sense of common responsibility to take action to address the challenges we face.

A comparative analytical frame

The process of reimagining a politics of antiracism and racial justice for the present needs to include more attention to mobilizations against racism both within and across national borders. It is also important that evolving research and policy debates are embedded in the everyday realities of both the Global North and the Global South. It is particularly important to pay attention to anti-colonial struggles that combined questions about national self-determination with broader struggles for justice and redistribution (Narayan 2019; Ogbar 2019; Slate 2012a; 2012b).

In the context of everyday politics and mobilizations, it is also possible that ideologies of antiracism can help to shape processes of othering and dehumanization. It is worth engaging here with a key point made by David Goldberg when he outlines the complex relationship between ideologies that seek to dehumanize Palestinians and the ways their treatment in turn reinforces forms of anti-Semitism:

Today, alongside the indiscriminate and inescapable targeting of animalized Palestinians, sometimes vicious and deadly anti-Semitisms are recharging. In the name of a self-preservation the value of which is deeply bruised by totalized targeting of the dispossessed, the drive to destroy Gazans and delimit Palestinians' life possibilities re-prompts and reinforces anti-Semitisms by those incensed by their dehumanizing treatment. (Goldberg 2015: 141)

While Goldberg's argument was developed very much in the context of the broader history of the conflict between Palestinians and Israel, the intense conflict that has followed the attacks and atrocities committed by Hamas on 7 October 2023 reinforces his argument. The period since the atrocities has been filled with both textual and visual images that rely on racialized images of Palestinians and Jewish Israelis, and with both traditional and new anti-Semitic tropes from all sections of the political spectrum.

This raises an important question that we need to address both theoretically and empirically in the coming period: namely, how do we think beyond race? But it is also important to note that, in contemporary discussions about how we may look beyond race and racism, there are signs of engaging with the question of how struggles against racism can tackle issues about our common humanity at the same time. We can see this in interventions by scholars such as Manuela Bojadžijev who outline a relational theory of racism that emphasizes the constant transformations and struggles around racism and antiracism, and the possibility of change that is part of those struggles (Bojadžijev 2020). It is also evident in the efforts of black feminist scholars such as Philomena Essed, who has argued that it is necessary to 'think through and beyond racism' in exploring the possibilities of seeing how struggles against racism can link up with broader hopes for tackling injustice and *dehumanization* in the world around us (Essed 2020).

Essed's effort to explore the complex intersections between efforts to tackle injustice and the need to develop an imaginary that allows us to look beyond racism is suggestive of the kinds of issues that we need to explore more fully in thinking about the challenges we face today.

It is to be hoped that future scholarly efforts in this field will be able to address the question of how we may begin to find hope that change can come about even in an environment that seems to allow little room for manoeuvre. This is certainly a conversation that needs to come to the fore in the conceptual and empirical research agendas that are emerging in the contemporary environment, since there is an urgent need to develop conversations about the future that can create possibilities for hope even in difficult times. This is evident in the narratives that have emerged in American society in the aftermath of the Black Lives Matter protests and mobilizations that seek to give voice to the possible ways in which healing and care can help to provide a source for hope for African Americans as well as the wider society (Harris 2023; Perry 2019).

Antiracism as the problem

In the contemporary environment where 'antiracism' has become a deeply contested term, both in the context of scholarly research and even more in public conversations, it is not surprising that we have seen a significant effort to construct antiracism as the problem, rather than racism as such. As a result, some public intellectuals, and researchers, have sought to frame antiracist activists and scholars as perhaps a greater danger to the search for racial justice and equality than racism and racialized exclusion. This has been a recurrent theme in some of the debates in the United States over the role that antiracism has played in political debates and in public culture.

Such critiques are by no means uniform, and range across the political spectrum, from left-wing efforts to centre discussion on the role of class inequalities to neo-conservative critics who seek to deny the role of racism in society. Although it would be wrong to see this strand of work as central to conversations about antiracism, it remains the case that efforts to construct antiracism as the problem have gained some traction in the context of contemporary conversations about race and related issues such as immigration in contemporary societies. Such arguments have been articulated by new right academics and intellectuals in the United States for some decades now, but in recent years we have seen interventions of a similar kind in other countries, including Britain and other European societies.

Many of these interventions are linked to new right ideologies, but it is also clear that some of the left are sceptical about the value of antiracism as a means of social change. One example of left critiques can be found in the work of Adolph Reed Jr, who seeks to question the ways in which key facets of antiracism lead away from any focus on class analysis or the role of the labour movement (Reed Jr 2017; 2018). For Reed, one of the striking absences in antiracist efforts to challenge racism in the present lies in the tendency to look to race-specific policy and political strategies rather than agendas that seek to bring the various sections of the working class together to struggle for social justice. He is particularly scathing about those critical race scholars who argue that nothing much has changed in terms of racism and racial inequality over the past century and more. From his perspective, this kind of argument remains silent on the struggles of all working people – regardless of race, gender, sexual orientation and immigration status – for social justice over this period. Although Reed's standpoint is somewhat marginal in much of the language of the left, related arguments have also been voiced by other scholars in relation to Black Lives Matter and other mobilizations, albeit from different intellectual perspectives (Johnson 2023; Johnson et al. 2022).

A more strident effort to question the role that antiracism plays in contemporary American society can be found in the work of both academic and public intellectuals from the liberal and neo-conservative right who see real dangers in what they perceive as a kind of *woke racism* linked to antiracist activists and mobilizations. One version of the focus on antiracism as a problem can be found in John McWhorter's critique of *woke racism*, which he defines in terms of key trends in what he sees as the various waves of American antiracism in the post-Civil Rights Movement period (McWhorter 2021). McWhorter is writing from a standpoint that he does not define as conservative, since he sees himself as an African American scholar who is concerned that antiracism has become a kind of secular religious ideology that works almost against the interests of the very people it is supposed to serve. Over the past decade or so we have also seen other efforts by both academics and public figures from African American backgrounds to distance themselves from versions of antiracism and racial thinking that do not address the needs of racialized minorities (Williams 2010; 2019).

While such voices are by no means the dominant ones within the broader conversations on race and antiracism, they do highlight a trend among some commentators, from both liberal and neo-conservative standpoints, to construct the problem as being antiracism rather than racism as such (Boyers, McWhorter and Williams 2023; Patterson et al. 2020). Such critiques are not necessarily interesting in terms of what they say about antiracism, but more in relation to what they say about the latest phase of the culture wars that come and go in the contemporary environment. But it would be wrong to ignore these kinds of interventions, from both the left and the right of the political spectrum, since it is crucial for antiracists to be able to engage in conversations about and be able to gather support for strategies that will allow for substantive changes in the structures of racism in our societies.

Will racism ever end?

A key part of ongoing academic and policy conversations about antiracism is framed around the question of how we can make progress, however unevenly and unpredictably, towards the eradication of racism in all its forms in the contemporary social and political environment. Although the terms of this discussion are always evolving and changing according to national and local contexts, it remains in many ways the key question that we need to come to terms with in any rounded analysis of antiracism and its impact on the contemporary context. It is the question that we shall engage with as we move to the conclusion of this book.

In the aftermath of mobilizations around Black Lives Matter, much of the attention has been on specific interventions and their direct or indirect impact on institutions such as the police. But it is also important to engage more with the question of how we can begin to address finding a way to develop a conversation around the creation of alliances across race, class and gender that can hold out the hope for change in the present, rather than leaving hope as a kind of aspiration for the future. This is a key part of the argument of radical scholars such as Cedric Johnson, who argue that in the aftermath of Black Lives Matter it would be a mistake to locate the possibility for change around a particular movement, since it is only through the formation of a majoritarian opposition that any hope for change in the present can be found (Johnson 2023). From this perspective, it is important not simply to see the possibilities for change through the lens of one movement or ideology but to look to the work that is being done on the ground by a wide range of movements and organizations to address racial injustices of the past and the present.

An important part of the challenge we face in the present can only be fully understood if we are able to comprehend and acknowledge the legacies that the messy histories of slavery, colonialism and racism have left us to deal with in our contemporary environment. This is an issue that has been highlighted in David Scott's account of the ways in which what he calls the 'irreparable evil' of plantation slavery has left enduring legacies in places such as the Caribbean that have proved difficult to repair or overcome in the present (Scott 2024). While Scott is not necessarily arguing that the 'irreparable evil' cannot be repaired in some way, he is suggesting that it is important that we should not lose sight either of the horrors of plantation slavery or of its ideological underpinnings and of its continuing impact on the contemporary societies in the Caribbean and beyond.

What such accounts suggest is that, in thinking about what it means to develop strategies for moving beyond racism, it is important to think about generalized changes in societies that can tackle inequalities at all levels, but also about the need to act in the present to address issues that are of immediate concern in relation to the persistence of racialized inequalities and divisions. But, as Marcus Hunter has argued in his powerful proposal in favour of the need for a radical programme of repair and healing in the United States, it is important to see 'radical reparations' as part of a process of recreating a nation that was from the beginning shaped by racism and slavery (Hunter 2024: 313–14).

What these accounts of the challenges we face suggest is that, at the most general level, it is important to explore the question of how we can determine whether a society is moving in the direction of tackling the structures of racialized inequality and injustice that have helped to shape both our history and the present. Whether we are looking at the situation in Europe,

North America, Brazil or South Africa, there are important issues to address and discuss as part of a conversation about how societies can move towards creating the conditions for racial justice and equity in the present and break with the legacies of past failures to substantively address this issue.

As I have argued earlier, it is important to avoid a simplistic dismissal of what has been achieved in the struggles against racism over the past few decades. While we can certainly be critical of the limits of existing policy and political agendas, it is also important to acknowledge the changes that have been brought about by interventions in key social and political arenas. While it may be difficult to gauge whether societies are, in a processual sense, moving to tackle racism and racialized inequalities, there are dangers in presenting racism as ever present and unchanging.

It is also important to develop an antiracist imaginary that can help us not just to think about the long histories of racism and exclusion, but to think about what the future may look like. It is important to acknowledge, as David Goldberg argues, that 'anti-racism requires not just being against the existing and past forms of racist expression, but doing so in the name of an affirming set of ideals – the dream – of what a society not driven by racial consideration in any (consequential) way would look like' (Goldberg 2015: 164). In thinking about what a society not shaped by race may look like, it is also necessary to address what the possibilities of hope may be, and how we can move in a more hopeful direction.

There is a tendency in the more pessimistic strands of critical race thinking to emphasize the permanence of racism, both historically and in the context of contemporary societies. This is evidenced in a number of interventions in the aftermath of the recent debates about Black Lives Matter that have argued forcefully that there has, if anything, been a retreat from earlier efforts to tackle racism in key institutional arenas, including education and employment (Rollock 2022; Warmington 2024).

These interventions can be seen to some extent as an expression of frustration at the pace of change that we have seen over the past few decades, and the efforts by neo-conservatives to question the need for any strategies of radical repair and reform. But there is a danger in these accounts that we can lose sight of the avenues for change that may be possible, and indeed the very possibility of radical avenues for change in the contemporary environment. From these perspectives, it seems implausible to envisage that racism will ever end or that we can progress towards societies where race as a category is not socially significant.

It is important in this context to hold on to the notion that those who have been subjected to racism, both historically and in the present, have never been simply objects and victims and have sought to resist and defend themselves in various ways. As Manuela Bojadžijev has argued, it is important to see antiracism as only to some extent tied to dominant ideas about race and subjugation since it is also part of wider political practices and struggles for change (Bojadžijev 2020). This is perhaps the main reason why it is important to link the development of a critical antiracist imaginary to both historical and empirical research that can help us assess and explore the possibilities for change in our societies today. In an environment where antiracism is the subject of intense critique from both the political left and right, it is important to pause, reflect and think about what the possibilities are for hope and optimism that we can develop the kinds of conversations that look forwards, and outline visions for a future where race plays no significant role in shaping social and political relations.

Rather than seeing antiracism as inevitably doomed to fail within the context of capitalist societies, it is important to explore the possibilities for antiracism to achieve both substantial and more limited changes that can impact on the quality of life of both individuals and communities. We need, in other words, to begin to reimagine what an antiracist society may look like, but also how we may be able to get there by bringing about changes and reforms in the societies in which we live today. We should remember, too, that the hope that the deep-seated structures of racism can be ended cannot remain a distant hope for a different society. It is important to locate strategies for ending racism in present-day societies, rather than framing hope in some distant future.

In attempting to think beyond racism and antiracism, it is important to engage fully with the complex realities of the evolving and changing racisms of the present. Research agendas and political and policy debates need to address the structural and everyday realities of racism. But it is equally important to develop research and policy conversations about how we can move beyond the politics of race. In framing these conversations, it is important to engage in detailed research into how a politics of antiracism can help us to move beyond racism. It is impressive that over the past few decades we have seen really exciting and innovative bodies of scholarship provide us with a much fuller understanding of the histories and processes that shaped racism in all its forms across the globe. It is equally vital that we engage in rigorous scholarship, research and conversations about the origins, development and impact of antiracism.

As we look forwards, it will be important for scholars, policy makers, politicians and activists to engage in the kind of open-ended conversations that can help us to provide a fuller understanding of the workings of antiracism as a force for change in the present. This needs a good measure of creativity, curiosity, humility and generosity as we develop research agendas that seek to address the question of how we can develop effective strategies for the elimination of racism in the world around us today. Rather than focusing nearly all of our attention on the histories of racism and the changing forms of racism today, we need to bring questions about antiracism more centrally into our research and conversations about how we move forwards to tackle both structural and other forms of racism in our societies. This is to some extent beginning to happen, particularly over the past two decades, as debates about mobilizations against racism have become an important component of scholarship. But, as I have also argued, there is a need to engage with the question of the way to develop research conversations about how we can move forwards in terms of policy and political agendas that tackle racialized inequalities and divisions in the world around us. This is particularly important at a time when there are clear frustrations about the limitations of efforts to tackle institutionalized racism and its consequences in contemporary societies.

References

Andersen, Margaret L. (2021) *Race in Society: The Enduring American Dilemma*. Second edition. Lanham: Rowman & Littlefield.

Andersen, Margaret L. and Collins, Patricia Hill (eds.) (2020) *Race, Class, and Gender: Intersections and Inequalities*. Tenth edition. Boston, MA: Cengage.

Angelou, Maya (1986) *And Still I Rise*. London: Virago.

Ansell, Amy E. (1997) *New Right, New Racism: Race and Reaction in the United States and Britain*. New York University Press.

Anthias, Floya and Lloyd, Cathie (eds.) (2002) *Rethinking Anti-Racisms: From Theory to Practice*. London: Routledge.

Aquino, Kristine (2017) *Racism and Resistance among the Filipino Diaspora: Everyday Anti-racism in Australia*. London: Taylor and Francis.

Aquino, Kristine (2020) 'Anti-Racism and Everyday Life' in J. Solomos (ed.) *Routledge International Handbook of Contemporary Racisms*, 216–29. London: Routledge.

Back, Les (2021) 'Hope's Work', *Antipode* 53, 1: 3–20.

Back, Les, Crabbe, Tim and Solomos, John (2001) *The Changing Face of Football: Racism, Identity and Multiculture in the English Game*. Oxford: Berg.

Back, Les, Keith, Michael, Shukra, Kalbir and Solomos, John (2023) *The Unfinished Politics of Race: Histories of Political Participation, Migration and Multiculturalism*. Cambridge University Press.

Back, Les and Mills, Kelly (2021) '"When You Score You're English, When You Miss You're Black": Euro 2020 and the Racial Politics of a

Penalty Shoot-Out', *Soundings: A Journal of Politics and Culture* 79: 110–21.

Back, Les and Solomos, John (1994) 'Labour and Racism: Trade Unions and the Selection of Parliamentary Candidates', *The Sociological Review* 42, 2: 165–201.

Badenoch, Kemi (2021) 'Minister for Equalities' Speech on the Commission on Race and Ethnic Disparities' Report'. www.gov.uk /government/speeches/minister-for-equalities-speech-on-the-com mission-on-race-and-ethnic-disparities-report.

Bakan, Abigail B. and Dua, Enakshi (eds.) (2014) *Theorizing Antiracism: Linkages in Marxism and Critical Race Theories.* University of Toronto Press.

Baker, Donald G. (1993) *Race, Ethnicity and Power: A Comparative Study.* London: Routledge & Kegan Paul.

Balibar, Étienne (2008) 'Racism Revisited: Sources, Relevance, and Aporias of a Modern Concept', *PMLA* 123, 5: 1630–9.

Balibar, Étienne and Wallerstein, Immanuel (1991) *Race, Nation, Class: Ambiguous Identities.* London: Verso.

Banton, Michael (1974) '1960: A Turning Point for the Study of Race Relations', *Daedalus* 103, 2: 31–44.

Banton, Michael (1998) *Racial Theories.* Cambridge University Press.

Barker, Martin (1981) *The New Racism: Conservatives and the Ideology of the Tribe.* London: Junction Books.

Bebber, Brett (2019) 'The Architects of Integration: Research, Public Policy, and the Institute of Race Relations in Post-imperial Britain', *Journal of Imperial and Commonwealth History* 48, 2: 319–50.

Becker, Elisabeth (2021) *Mosques in the Metropolis: Incivility, Caste, and Contention in Europe.* University of Chicago Press.

Ben-Tovim, Gideon, Gabriel, John, Law, Ian and Stredder, Kathleen (1986) *The Local Politics of Race.* Basingstoke: Macmillan.

Benhabib, Seyla (2004) *The Rights of Others: Aliens, Residents and Citizens.* Cambridge University Press.

Bhattacharyya, Gargi, Elliott-Cooper, Adam, Balana, Sita, et al. (2021) *Empire's Endgame: Racism and the British State.* London: Pluto Press.

Bhattacharyya, Gargi, Virdee, Satnam and Winter, Aaron (2020) 'Revisiting Histories of Anti-racist Thought and Activism', *Identities: Global Studies in Culture and Power* 27, 1: 1–19.

Blain, Keisha N. (2018) *Set the World on Fire: Black Nationalist Women and the Global Struggle for Freedom.* Philadelphia: University of Pennsylvania Press.

Blain, Keisha N. (2024) *Wake Up America: Black Women on the Future of Democracy.* New York: W. W. Norton.

Blake, Felice, Ioanide, Paula and Reed, Alison (eds.) (2019) *Antiracism Inc.: Why the Way We Talk about Racial Justice Matters*. Santa Barbara, CA: Punctum Books.

Bloch, Alice, Neal, Sarah and Solomos, John (2013) *Race, Multiculture & Social Policy*. Basingstoke: Palgrave Macmillan.

Bloomfield, Jon (2019) *Our City: Migrants and the Making of Modern Birmingham*. London: Unbound.

Bojadžijev, Manuela (2020) 'Anti-racism as Method' in J. Solomos (ed.) *Routledge International Handbook of Contemporary Racisms*, 193–204. London: Routledge.

Bonnett, Alastair (1993) *Radicalism, Anti-racism, and Representation*. London: Routledge.

Bonnett, Alastair (2000) *Anti-Racism*. London: Routledge.

Bonnett, Alastair (2022) *Multiracism: Rethinking Racism in Global Context*. Cambridge: Polity.

Bourne, Jenny (2016) 'When Black Was a Political Colour: A Guide to the Literature', *Race & Class* 58, 1: 122–30.

Boutros, Magda (2024) 'Antiracism without Races: How Activists Produce Knowledge about Race and Policing in France', *Social Problems* 71, 1: 1–17.

Boyers, Robert, McWhorter, John and Williams, Thomas Chatterton (2023) 'Talking Race Matters: A Conversation with John McWhorter & Thomas Chatterton Williams', *Salmagundi – A Quarterly of the Humanities and Social Sciences* 218–19: 62–81, 227.

Braverman, Suella (2023a) 'Speech on the Failure of Multiculturalism', https://metro.co.uk/2023/09/26/suella-braverman-speech-america -global-asylum-rules-refugee-convention-19560681.

Braverman, Suella (2023b) 'Speech to 2023 Conservative Party Conference', www.google.com/search?q=suella+braverman+speech+ to+2023+Conservative+Party+conference&oq=suella+braverman+ speech+to+2023+Conservative+Party+conference&gs_lcrp=EgZjaH JvbWUyBggAEEUYOTIGCAEQIRgKMgcIAhAhGI8CMgcIAxAhGI 8C0gEJMjAwNTFqMGo3qAIAsAIA&sourceid=chrome&ie=UTF-8, 3 October 2023.

Brown, Nadia E. (2014) *Sisters in the Statehouse: Black Women and Legislative Decision Making*. Oxford University Press.

Cell, J. W. (1982) *The Highest Stage of White Supremacy: The Origins of Segregation in South Africa and the American South*. Cambridge University Press.

Chatelain, Marcia (2019) 'Five Years after Ferguson', *Dissent* 66, 4: 127–32.

Christerson, Brad, Salvatierra, Alexia, Romero, Robert Chao and Yuen,

Nancy Wang (2023) *God's Resistance: Mobilizing Faith to Defend Immigrants*. New York University Press.

Church Commissioners for England (2023) *Church Commissioners' Research into Historic Links to Transatlantic Chattel Slavery*. London: Church Commissioners for England.

Cobb, Jelani (2020) *The Substance of Hope: Barack Obama and the Paradox of Progress*. New York: Bloomsbury Publishing.

Collins, Patricia Hill (2024) *Lethal Intersections: Race, Gender, and Violence*. Cambridge: Polity.

Comaroff, John L. (1998) 'Reflections on the Colonial State, in South Africa and Elsewhere: Factions, Fragments, Facts and Fictions', *Social Identities* 4, 3: 321–61.

Commission on Race and Ethnic Disparities (2021) *The Report*. London: Commission on Race and Ethnic Disparities.

Connell, Kieran (2019) *Black Handsworth: Race in 1980s Britain*. Oakland: University of California Press.

Crenshaw, Kimberlé Williams (2019a) 'How Colorblindness Flourished in the Age of Obama' in K. W. Crenshaw, L. C. Harris, D. HoSang and G. Lipsitz (eds.) *Seeing Race Again: Countering Colorblindness across the Disciplines*, 128–54. Oakland: University of California Press.

Crenshaw, Kimberlé Williams (2019b) 'Unmasking Colorblindness in the Law: Lessons from the Formation of Critical Race Theory' in K. W. Crenshaw, L. C. Harris, D. HoSang and G. Lipsitz (eds.) *Seeing Race Again: Countering Colorblindness across the Disciplines*, 52–84, Oakland: University of California Press.

Darling, Jonathan and Bauder, Harald (eds.) (2019) *Sanctuary Cities and Urban Struggles: Rescaling Migration, Citizenship, and Rights*. Manchester University Press.

Davis, Joshua T. and Perry, Samuel L. (2021) 'White Christian Nationalism and Relative Political Tolerance for Racists', *Social Problems* 68, 3: 513–34.

Dawson, Michael C. (1994) *Behind the Mule: Race and Class in African-American Politics*. Princeton University Press.

Dawson, Michael C. (2011) *Not in Our Lifetimes: The Future of Black Politics*. University of Chicago Press.

Dawson, Michael C. (2014) 'The Hollow Shell: Loïc Wacquant's Vision of State, Race and Economics', *Ethnic and Racial Studies* 37, 10: 1767–75.

Dawson, Michael C. and Francis, Megan Ming (2015) 'Black Politics and the Neoliberal Racial Order', *Public Culture* 78: 23–62.

Desmond, Matthew and Emirbayer, Mustafa (2015) *Race in America*. New York: W. W. Norton & Company.

Dixon, Kevin, Cashmore, Ellis and Cleland, Jamie (2022) '"A Little Less Conversation": An Exploration of Soccer Fan Attitudes towards "The Knee" Protest and the Anti-racism Message', *Soccer & Society* 24, 5: 698–711.

Dubois, Laurent (2012) *Haiti: The Aftershocks of History*. New York: Metropolitan Books.

Eatwell, Roger and Goodwin, Matthew J. (2018) *National Populism: The Revolt against Liberal Democracy*. London: Pelican.

Ehsan, Rakib (2023) *Beyond Grievance: What the Left Gets Wrong about Ethnic Minorities*. London: Forum.

Elias, Amanuel, Ben, Jehonathan and Hiruy, Kiros (2023) 'Re-imagining Anti-racism as a Core Organisational Value', *Australian Journal of Management* 49, 1: 15–32.

Essed, Philomena (2020) 'Humiliation, Dehumanization and the Quest for Dignity: Researching beyond Racism' in J. Solomos (ed.) *Routledge International Handbook of Contemporary Racisms*, 442–55. London: Routledge.

Fairfax, Lisa M. (2022) 'Racial Rhetoric or Reality? Cautious Optimism on the Link between Corporate #BLM Speech and Behavior', *Columbia Business Law Review* 2022, 120–205.

Favell, Adrian (2001) 'Multi-ethnic Britain: An Exception in Europe?' *Patterns of Prejudice* 35, 1: 35–57.

Fella, Stefano and Ruzza, Carlo (eds.) (2013) *Anti-racist Movements in the EU: Between Europeanisation and National Trajectories*. Basingstoke: Palgrave Macmillan.

Ferguson, Annie (2023) 'Redefining Antiracism: Learning from Activists to Sharpen Academic Language', *Sociology Compass* 17, 1.

Finney, Nissa, Nazroo, James Y., Bécares, Laia, Kapadia, Dharmi and Shlomo, Natalie (2023) *Racism and Ethnic Inequality in a Time of Crisis: Findings from the Evidence for Equality National Survey*. Bristol: Policy Press.

Fogelson, Robert M., Black, Gordon S. and Lipsky, Michael (1969) 'Report of the National Advisory Commission on Civil Disorders', *American Political Science Review* 63, 4: 1269–81.

Francis, Megan Ming and Wright-Rigueur, Leah (2021) 'Black Lives Matter in Historical Perspective', *Annual Review of Law and Social Science* 17, 1: 441–58.

Frank, Sybille and Ristic, Mirjana (2020) 'Urban Fallism: Monuments, Iconoclasm and Activism', *City* 24, 3–4: 552–64.

Fredrickson, George M. (1981) *White Supremacy: A Comparative Study In American and South African History*. New York: Oxford Unversity Press.

Fredrickson, George M. (1997) *The Comparative Imagination: On the History of Racism, Nationalism and Social Movements*. Berkeley: University of California Press.

Fredrickson, George M. (1998) *Black Liberation: A Comparative History of Black Ideologies in the United States and South Africa*. New York: Oxford University Press.

Fredrickson, George M. (2002) *Racism: A Short History*. Princeton University Press.

Frisina, Annalisa and Hawthorne, Camilla A. (2017) 'Italians with Veils and Afros: Gender, Beauty, and the Everyday Anti-racism of the Daughters of Immigrants in Italy', *Journal of Ethnic and Migration Studies* 44, 5: 718–35.

Frisina, Annalisa and Kyeremeh, Sandra Agyei (2022) 'Music and Words against Racism: A Qualitative Study with Racialized Artists in Italy,' *Ethnic and Racial Studies* 45, 15: 2913–33.

Furedi, Frank (2018) *Populism and the European Culture Wars: The Conflict of Values between Hungary and the EU*. London: Routledge.

Furedi, Frank (2021) *Why Borders Matter: Why Humanity Must Relearn the Art of Drawing Boundaries*. London: Routledge.

Gaines, Kevin (1996) *Uplifting the Race: Black Leadership, Politics and Culture in the Twentieth Century*. Chapel Hill: University of North Carolina Press.

George, Erika (2021) 'Racism as a Human Rights Risk: Reconsidering the Corporate "Responsibility to Respect" Rights', *Business and Human Rights Journal* 6, 3: 576–83.

Georgiou, Myria (2017) 'Is London Open? Mediating and Ordering Cosmopolitanism in Crisis', *International Communication Gazette* 79, 6–7: 636–55.

Georgiou, Myria, Hall, Suzanne M. and Dajani, Deena (2022) 'Suspension: Disabling the City of Refuge?' *Journal of Ethnic and Migration Studies* 48, 9: 2206–22.

Gilroy, Paul (1987) *There Ain't No Black in the Union Jack: The Cultural Politics of Race and Nation*. London: Hutchinson.

Gilroy, Paul (2004) *After Empire: Melancholia or Convivial Culture?* London: Routledge.

Gilroy, Paul (2018) '"Where Every Breeze Speaks of Courage and Liberty": Offshore Humanism and Marine Xenology, or, Racism and the Problem of Critique at Sea Level', *Antipode* 50, 1: 3–22.

Gilroy, Paul (2019) *Never Again: Refusing Race and Salvaging the Human*. Bergen: Holberg Prize.

Gilroy, Paul (2022) 'Antiracism, Blue Humanism and the Black Mediterranean', *Transition* 132: 108–22.

Gilroy, Paul and Oriogun-Williams, Femi (2021) 'The Possibility of a Creolised Planet', *Soundings: A Journal of Politics and Culture* 78: 124–37.

Gilroy, Paul, Sandset, Tony, Bangstad, Sindre and Høibjerg, Gard Ringen (2018) 'A Diagnosis of Contemporary Forms of Racism, Race and Nationalism: A Conversation with Professor Paul Gilroy', *Cultural Studies* 33, 2: 173–97.

Givens, Terri E. (2021) *Radical Empathy: Finding a Path to Bridging Racial Divides*. Bristol: Policy Press.

Glaude, Eddie S. (2020) *Begin Again: James Baldwin's America and Its Urgent Lessons for Our Own*. New York: Crown.

Golash-Boza, Tanya Maria (2015) *Race & Racisms: A Critical Approach*. New York: Oxford University Press.

Golash-Boza, Tanya Maria (2016) *Race & Racisms: A Critical Approach. Brief Edition*. New York: Oxford University Press.

Goldberg, David Theo (2006) 'Racial Europeanization', *Ethnic and Racial Studies* 29, 2: 331–64.

Goldberg, David Theo (2009) *The Threat of Race: Reflections on Racial Neoliberalism*. Malden, MA: Wiley Blackwell.

Goldberg, David Theo (2015) *Are We All Postracial Yet?* Cambridge: Polity.

Goldberg, David Theo (2021) 'The War on Critical Race Theory', *Boston Review*, http://bostonreview.net/race-politics/david-theo-goldberg -war-critical-race-theory, 7 May 2021.

Goldberg, David Theo and Giroux, Susan Searls (2014) *Sites of Race: Conversations with Susan Searls Giroux*. Cambridge: Polity.

Goodhart, David (2013) *The British Dream: Successes and Failures of Post-war Immigration*. London: Atlantic.

Goodhart, David (2017) *The Road to Somewhere: The Populist Revolt and the Future of Politics*. London: C. Hurst & Company.

Goodhart, David (2019) 'Wishful Thinking and Unresolved Tensions', *Ethnicities* 19, 6: 983–90.

Gooding-Williams, Robert, Goldberg, David Theo, Hooker, Juliet and Hanchard, Michael G. (2020) 'Democracy's History of Inegalitarianism: Symposium on Michael Hanchard, *The Spectre of Race: How Discrimination Haunts Western Democracy*', *Political Theory* 48, 3: 357–77.

Goodwin, Matthew J. (2023) *Values, Voice and Virtue: The New British Politics*. London: Penguin Books.

Gorski, Paul C. (2018a) 'Fighting Racism, Battling Burnout: Causes of Activist Burnout in US Racial Justice Activists', *Ethnic and Racial Studies* 42, 5: 667–87.

Gorski, Paul C. (2018b) 'Racial Battle Fatigue and Activist Burnout in Racial Justice Activists of Color at Predominately White Colleges and Universities', *Race Ethnicity and Education* 22, 1: 1–20.

Hage, Ghassan (2015) 'Recalling Anti-racism', *Ethnic and Racial Studies* 39, 1: 123–33.

Hall, Stuart (1980) 'Race, Articulation and Societies Structured in Dominance' in United Nations Educational, Scientific and Cultural Organization (ed.) *Sociological Theories: Race and Colonialism*, 305–45. Paris: United Nations Educational, Scientific and Cultural Organization.

Hall, Stuart (2017) *Fateful Triangle: Race, Ethnicity, Nation*. Cambridge, MA: Harvard University Press.

Hall, Stuart, Gilroy, Paul and Gilmore, Ruth Wilson (eds.) (2021) *Selected Writings on Race and Difference*. Durham, NC: Duke University Press.

Hamilton, Charles V., Hultley, Lynn, Alexander, Neville, Guimarães, Antonio Sergio and James, Wilmot (eds.) (2001) *Beyond Racism: Race and Inequality in Brazil, South Africa, and the United States*. Boulder: Lynne Rienner Publishers.

Han, Hahrie and Arora, Maneesh (2022) 'Igniting Change: An Evangelical Megachurch's Racial Justice Program', *Perspectives on Politics* 20, 4: 1260–74.

Hanchard, Michael G. (1994) *Orpheus and Power: The Movimento Negro of Rio de Janeiro and Sao Paulo, Brazil, 1945–1988*. Princeton University Press.

Hanchard, Michael G. (2010) 'Contours of Black Political Thought: An Introduction and Perspective', *Political Theory* 38, 4: 510–36.

Hanchard, Michael G. (2018) *The Spectre of Race: How Discrimination Haunts Western Democracy*. Princeton University Press.

Harris, Christopher Paul (2023) *To Build a Black Future: The Radical Politics of Joy, Pain, and Care*. Princeton University Press.

Harris, Scarlet (2021) 'Islamophobia, Anti-racism and the British Left: Muslim Activists as "Racialised Outsiders"', *Journal of Ethnic and Migration Studies* 48, 13: 3078–94.

Harvard University, Presidential Committee on Harvard and the Legacy of Slavery (2022) *The Legacy of Slavery at Harvard: Report and Recommendations of the Presidential Committee*. Cambridge, MA: Harvard University Press.

Hawthorne, Camilla A. (2017) 'In Search of Black Italia: Notes on Race, Belonging, and Activism in the Black Mediterranean', *Transition* 123: 152–74.

Hawthorne, Camilla A. (2022) *Contesting Race and Citizenship: Youth*

Politics in the Black Mediterranean. Ithaca, NY: Cornell University Press.

Hawthorne, Camilla A. and Lewis, Jovan Scott (eds.) (2023) *The Black Geographic: Praxis, Resistance, Futurity.* Durham, NC: Duke University Press.

Hayward, Clarissa Rile, Threadcraft, Shatema, Lebron, Christopher J. and Shelby, Tommie (2019) 'The Demand of Justice: Symposium on Tommie Shelby's *Dark Ghettos: Injustice, Dissent, and Reform,* Harvard University Press, 2016', *Political Theory* 47, 4: 527–57.

Hazard Jr, Anthony Q. (2012) *Postwar Anti-racism: The United States, UNESCO, and 'Race', 1945–1968.* New York: Palgrave Macmillan.

Hesse, Barnor (2004) 'Im/plausible Deniability: Racism's Conceptual Double Bind', *Social Identities* 10, 1: 9–29.

Hesse, Barnor (2007) 'Racialized Modernity: An Analytics of White Mythologies', *Ethnic and Racial Studies* 30, 4: 643–63.

Hesse, Barnor and Hooker, Juliet (2017) 'Introduction: On Black Political Thought inside Global Black Protest', *South Atlantic Quarterly* 116, 3: 443–56.

Hooker, Juliet (2016) 'Black Lives Matter and the Paradoxes of U.S. Black Politics: From Democratic Sacrifice to Democratic Repair', *Political Theory* 44, 4: 448–69.

Hooker, Juliet (2017) 'Black Protest / White Grievance: On the Problem of White Political Imaginations Not Shaped by Loss', *South Atlantic Quarterly* 116, 3: 483–504.

HoSang, Daniel Martinez (2019) 'A Wider Type of Freedom' in F. Blake, P. Ioanide and A. Reed (eds.) *Antiracism Inc.: Why the Way We Talk about Racial Justice Matters,* 57–79, Goleta, CA: Punctum Books.

HoSang, Daniel Martinez (2021) *A Wider Type of Freedom: How Struggles for Racial Justice Liberate Everyone.* Oakland: University of California Press.

Houghteling, Clara and Dantzler, Prentiss A. (2020) 'Taking a Knee, Taking a Stand: Social Networks and Identity Salience in the 2017 NFL Protests', *Sociology of Race and Ethnicity* 6, 3: 396–415.

House of Commons, House of Lords, Joint Committee on Human Rights (2020) *Black People, Racism and Human Rights, Eleventh Report of Session 2019–21.* London: House of Commons.

Humphris, Rachel (2023) 'Sanctuary City as Mobilising Metaphor: How Sanctuary Articulates Urban Governance', *Journal of Ethnic and Migration Studies* 49, 14: 3585–601.

Hunter, Marcus Anthony (2024) *Radical Reparations: Healing the Soul of a Nation.* New York: Amistad.

Johnson, Cedric (2023) *After Black Lives Matter: Policing and Anti-Capitalist Struggle*. London: Verso.

Johnson, Cedric, Chibber, Vivek, Arena, John, White, Mia, Reed, Touré F. and Moody, Kim (2022) *The Panthers Can't Save Us Now: Debating Left Politics and Black Lives Matter*. London: Verso.

Joseph-Salisbury, Remi and Connelly, Laura (2021) *Anti-racist Scholar-Activism*. Manchester University Press.

Kassimeris, Christos, Lawrence, Stefan and Pipini, Magdalini (2022) 'Racism in Football', *Soccer & Society* 23, 8: 824–33.

Katz, Judith (1978) *White Awareness: Handbook for Anti-racism Training*. Norman: University of Oklahoma Press.

Kaufmann, Eric P. (2017) *'Racial Self-Interest' Is Not Racism: Ethno-demographic Interests and the Immigration Debate*. London: Policy Exchange.

Kaufmann, Eric P. (2018) *Whiteshift: Populism, Immigration and the Future of White Majorities*. London: Penguin.

Kelley, Robin D. G. (1994) *Race Rebels: Culture, Politics, and the Black Working Class*. New York: Free Press.

Kelley, Robin D. G. (2022) *Freedom Dreams: The Black Radical Imagination*. Twentieth anniversary, revised and expanded edition. Boston: Beacon Press.

Kerner Commission (2016) *The Kerner Report: The National Advisory Commission on Civil Disorders*. Princeton University Press.

Keskinen, Suvi, Alemanji, Aminkeng Atabong and Seikkula, Minna (eds.) (2024) *Race, Bordering and Disobedient Knowledge: Activism and Everyday Struggles in Europe*. Manchester University Press.

Kick it Out (2023) *30 Year Impact Report*. Nuneaton: Kick it Out.

King, Desmond S. and Smith, Rogers M. (2011) *Still a House Divided: Race and Politics in Obama's America*. Princeton University Press.

Knowles, Caroline (2003) *Race and Social Analysis*. London: SAGE.

Kowal, Emma, Franklin, Hayley and Paradies, Yin (2013) 'Reflexive Antiracism: A Novel Approach to Diversity Training', *Ethnicities* 13, 3: 316–37.

Kundnani, Arun (2023) *What Is Antiracism? And Why It Means Anticapitalism*. London: Verso.

Lamont, Michèle, Silva, Graziella Moraes, Welburn, Jessica, et al. (2016) *Getting Respect: Responding to Stigma and Discrimination in the United States, Brazil, and Israel*. Princeton University Press.

Lasch-Quinn, Elisabeth (1996) 'Radical Chic and the Rise of Therapeutics of Race', *Salmagundi – A Quarterly of the Humanities and Social Sciences* 112: 8–25.

Lasch-Quinn, Elisabeth (2001) *Race Experts: How Racial Etiquette, Sensitivity Training, and New Age Therapy Hijacked the Civil Rights Revolution*. New York: Norton.

Lawrence, Bonita and Dua, Enakshi (2005) 'Decolonizing Antiracism', *Social Justice* 32, 4: 120–43.

Lebron, Christopher J. (2017) *The Making of Black Lives Matter: A Brief History of an Idea*. New York: Oxford University Press.

Lentin, Alana (2000) '"Race", Racism and Anti-racism: Challenging Contemporary Classifications', *Social Identities* 6, 1: 91–106.

Lentin, Alana (2004a) 'Racial States, Anti-racist Responses: Picking Holes in "Culture" and "Human Rights"', *European Journal of Social Theory* 7, 4: 427–43.

Lentin, Alana (2004b) *Racism and Anti-racism in Europe*. London: Pluto Press.

Lentin, Alana (2020) *Why Race Still Matters*. Cambridge: Polity.

Levenson, Zachary and Paret, Marcel (2023) 'The South African Tradition of Racial Capitalism', *Ethnic and Racial Studies* 46, 16: 3403–24.

Lewis, Russell (1988) *Anti-racism: A Mania Exposed*. London: Quartet.

Lipsitz, George (2019) 'The Logic of "Illogical" Opposition: Tools and Tactics for Tough Times' in F. Blake, P. Ioanide and A. Reed (eds.) *Antiracism Inc.: Why the Way We Talk about Racial Justice Matters*, 273–93. Goleta, CA: Punctum Books.

Lloyd, Cathie (1998) *Discourses of Antiracism in France*. Aldershot: Ashgate.

Lopez Bunyasi, Tehama and Smith, Candis Watts (2019) 'Do All Black Lives Matter Equally to Black People? Respectability Politics and the Limitations of Linked Fate', *Journal of Race, Ethnicity, and Politics* 4, 1: 180–215.

Macpherson, William (1999) *The Stephen Lawrence Inquiry: Report of an Inquiry by Sir William Macpherson of Cluny*. London: Stationery Office.

Makalani, Minkah (2011) *In the Cause of Freedom: Radical Black Internationalism from Harlem to London, 1917–1939*. Chapel Hill: University of North Carolina Press.

Makalani, Minkah (2017) 'Black Lives Matter and the Limits of Formal Black Politics', *South Atlantic Quarterly* 116, 3: 529–52.

Malik, Kenan (2023) *Not So Black and White: A History of Race from White Supremacy to Identity Politics*. London: C. Hurst & Company.

Martiniello, Marco (2018) 'Local Communities of Artistic Practices and the Slow Emergence of a "Post-racial" Generation', *Ethnic and Racial Studies* 41, 6: 1146–62.

Mbembe, Achille (2017) *Critique of Black Reason*. Durham, NC: Duke University Press.

McClain, Paula Denice and Johnson, Jessica D. (2018) '*Can We All Get Along?*': *Racial and Ethnic Minorities in American Politics*. Seventh edition. New York: Westview Press.

McClain, Paula Denice and Tauber, Steven C. (2018) *American Government in Black and White: Diversity and Democracy*. Third edition. New York: Oxford University Press.

McLaughlin, Eugene and Neal, Sarah (2007) 'Who Can Speak to Race and Nation? Intellectuals, Public Policy Formation and the Future of Multi-ethnic Britain Commission', *Cultural Studies* 21, 6: 910–30.

McNeil, Daniel (2023) *Thinking while Black: Translating the Politics and Popular Culture*. New Brunswick: Rutgers University Press.

McWhorter, John H. (2021) *Woke Racism: How a New Religion Has Betrayed Black America*. New York: Portfolio/Penguin.

Meer, Nasar (2022) *The Cruel Optimism of Racial Justice*. Bristol: Policy Press.

Meer, Nasar (2023) 'Revisiting the Cruel Optimism of Racial Justice – A Response to Fadil, Favell and St Louis', *Ethnicities* 23, 6: 980–5.

Meghji, Ali and Niang, Sophie Marie (2022) 'Between Post-racial Ideology and Provincial Universalisms: Critical Race Theory, Decolonial Thought and COVID-19 in Britain', *Sociology* 56, 1: 131–47.

Mills, Charles W. (2017) *Black Rights / White Wrongs: The Critique of Racial Liberalism*. New York: Oxford University Press.

Mills, Charles W. (2020) 'The Racial State' in J. Solomos (ed.) *Routledge International Handbook of Contemporary Racisms*, 99–109. London: Routledge.

Minister of State for Equalities (2022) *Inclusive Britain: Government Response to the Commission on Race and Ethnic Disparities*. London: HMSO.

Montagu, Ashley (1972) *Statement on Race: An Annotated Elaboration and Exposition of the Four Statements on Race Issued by the United Nations Educational, Scientific, and Cultural Organization*. Third edition. New York: Oxford University Press.

Moreno Figueroa, Monica G. and Wade, Peter (eds.) (2022) *Against Racism: Organizing for Social Change in Latin America*. University of Pittsburgh Press.

Mosse, George L. (1985) *Toward the Final Solution: A History of European Racism*. Madison: University of Wisconsin Press.

Mullen, Stephen and Newman, Simon P. (2018) *Slavery, Abolition and the University of Glasgow: Report and Recommendations of the University of Glasgow History of Slavery Steering Committee.* University of Glasgow.

Murray, Douglas (2017) *The Strange Death of Europe: Immigration, Identity, Islam.* London: Bloomsbury Continuum.

Murray, Douglas (2019) *The Madness of Crowds: Gender, Identity, Morality.* London: Bloomsbury Continuum.

Narayan, John (2019) 'British Black Power: The Anti-imperialism of Political Blackness and the Problem of Nativist Socialism', *The Sociological Review* 67, 5: 945–67.

Nash, Jennifer C. (2019) *Black Feminism Reimagined: After Intersectionality.* Durham, NC: Duke University Press.

Nelson, Alondra (2011) *Body and Soul: The Black Panther Party and the Fight against Medical Discrimination.* Minneapolis: University of Minnesota Press.

Nelson, Jacqueline and Dunn, Kevin (2017) 'Neoliberal Anti-racism: Responding to "Everywhere but Different" Racism', *Progress in Human Geography* 41, 1: 26–43.

O'Brien, Eileen (2009) 'From Antiracism to Antiracisms', *Sociology Compass* 3, 3: 501–12.

Ogbar, Jeffrey O. G. (2019) *Black Power: Radical Politics and African American Identity.* Baltimore: Johns Hopkins University Press.

Olney, Charles (2021) 'Black Lives Matter and the Politics of Redemption', *Philosophy & Social Criticism.*

Ostertag, Stephen F. (2019) 'Antiracism Movements and the US Civil Sphere: The Case of Black Lives Matter' in J. Alexander, T. Stack and F. Khosrokhavar (eds.) *Breaching the Civil Order: Radicalism and the Civil Sphere*, 70–91. Cambridge University Press.

Owolade, Tomiwa (2023) *This Is Not America: Why Black Lives in Britain Matter.* London: Atlantic Books.

Palmer, Frank (1986) *Anti-racism: An Assault on Education and Value.* London: Sherwood Press.

Parekh, Bhikhu (2000) *The Future of Multi-Ethnic Britain: Report of the Commission on the Future of Multi-Ethnic Britain.* London: Profile Books.

Patterson, Orlando, Jefferson, Margo, McWhorter, John, Pinckney, Darryl and Williams, Thomas Chatterton (2020) 'The Black Intellectual & the Condition of the Culture', *Salmagundi – A Quarterly of the Humanities and Social Sciences* 206–7: 124–273.

Paul, Joshua (2013) 'Post-racial Futures: Imagining Post-racialist Anti-racism(s)', *Ethnic and Racial Studies* 37, 4: 702–18.

Paul, Joshua (2020) '"Actually What Is Happening Is that These Constructs Are Being Built for Us": Appraising the Status and Future of Race in Progressive Political Struggle', *Identities: Global Studies in Culture and Power* 29, 5: 614–32.

Penfold, Connor and Cleland, Jamie (2022) 'Kicking It Out? Football Fans' Views of Anti-racism Initiatives in English Football', *Journal of Sport and Social Issues* 46, 2: 176–98.

Perry, Imani (2019) *Breathe: A Letter to My Sons*. Boston: Beacon Press.

Perry, Kennetta Hammond (2016) *London Is the Place for Me: Black Britons, Citizenship and the Politics of Race*. Oxford University Press.

Pettigrew, Thomas F. (2009) 'Post Racism? Putting President Obama's Victory in Perspective', *Du Bois Review: Social Science Research on Race* 6, 2: 279–92.

Piketty, Thomas (2014) *Capital in the Twenty-First Century*. Cambridge, MA: The Belknap Press of Harvard University Press.

Ramirez, Steven A. (2023) 'A Vision of the Anti-racist Public Corporation', *University of Cincinnati Law Review* 91, 3: 828–69.

Reed Jr, Adolph L. (2016) 'The Post-1965 Trajectory of Race, Class, and Urban Politics in the United States Reconsidered', *Labor Studies Journal* 41, 3: 260–91.

Reed Jr, Adolph L. (2017) 'The Kerner Commission and the Irony of Antiracist Politics', *Labor: Studies in Working-Class History of the Americas* 14, 4: 31–8.

Reed Jr, Adolph L. (2018) 'Antiracism: A Neoliberal Alternative to a Left', *Dialectical Anthropology* 42, 2: 105–15.

Renton, David (2018) *Never Again: Rock Against Racism and the Anti-Nazi League 1976–1982*. London: Routledge.

Rollock, Nicola (2022) *The Racial Code: Tales of Resistance and Survival*. London: Allen Lane.

Rose, Eliot Joseph Benn (1968) 'The Institute's "Survey of Race Relations in Britain": A Report on Four Years' Progress', *Race* 9, 4: 511–20.

Rose, Eliot Joseph Benn (1969) *Colour & Citizenship: A Report on British Race Relations*. Oxford University Press.

Santow, Mark E. (2023) *Saul Alinsky and the Dilemmas of Race: Community Organizing in the Postwar City*. University of Chicago Press.

Savage, Mike (2021) *The Return of Inequality: Social Change and the Weight of the Past*. Cambridge, MA: Harvard University Press.

Sayyid, Salman (2017) 'Post-racial Paradoxes: Rethinking European Racism and Anti-racism'. *Patterns of Prejudice* 51, 1: 9–25.

Scarman, Lord (1981) *The Brixton Disorders 10–12 April 1981: Report of an Inquiry by the Rt. Hon. The Lord Scarman OBE*. London: HMSO.

Scott, David (2024) *Irreparable Evil: An Essay in Moral and Reparatory History*. New York: Columbia University Press.

Scott, Jamil S. and Brown, Nadia E. (2016) 'Scholarship on #BlackLivesMatter and Its Implications on Local Electoral Politics', *Politics, Groups, and Identities* 4, 4: 702–8.

Seikkula, Minna (2022) 'Affirming or Contesting White Innocence? Anti-racism Frames in Grassroots Activists' Accounts', *Ethnic and Racial Studies* 45, 5: 789–808.

Shafi, Azfar and Nagdee, Ilyas (2022) *Race to the Bottom: Reclaiming Antiracism*. London: Pluto Press.

Shepherd, Nick (2020) 'After the #Fall: The Shadow of Cecil Rhodes at the University of Cape Town', *City* 24, 3–4: 565–79.

Silva, Antonio José Bacelar da (2022) *Between Brown and Black: Antiracist Activism in Brazil*. New Brunswick, NJ: Rutgers University Press.

Silva, Graziella Moraes (2012) 'Folk Conceptualizations of Racism and Antiracism in Brazil and South Africa', *Ethnic and Racial Studies* 35, 3: 506–22.

Slate, Nico (2012a) *Colored Cosmopolitanism: The Shared Struggle for Freedom in the United States and India*. Cambridge, MA: Harvard University Press.

Slate, Nico (ed.) (2012b) *Black Power beyond Borders: The Global Dimensions of the Black Power Movement*. London: Palgrave Macmillan.

Smith, Rogers M. and King, Desmond (2021) 'Racial Reparations against White Protectionism: America's New Racial Politics', *Journal of Race, Ethnicity, and Politics* 6, 1: 82–96.

Smith, Rogers M. and King, Desmond (2024) *America's New Racial Battle Lines: Protect versus Repair*. University of Chicago Press.

Smith, Rogers M. and King, Desmond S. (2009) 'Barack Obama and the Future of American Racial Politics', *Du Bois Review: Social Science Research on Race* 6, 1: 25–35.

Solomos, John (ed.) (2020) *Routledge International Handbook of Contemporary Racisms*. Abingdon: Routledge.

Solomos, John (2023) *Race, Ethnicity and Social Theory*. London: Routledge.

Solomos, John and Back, Les (1995) *Race, Politics and Social Change*. London: Routledge.

Sowell, Thomas (1981) *Markets and Minorities*. Oxford: Basil Blackwell.

Sowell, Thomas (2013) *Intellectuals and Race*. New York: Basic Books.

Srivastava, Sarita (2024) *'Are You Calling Me a Racist?' Why We Need to Stop Talking about Race and Start Making Real Antiracist Change*. New York University Press.

St Louis, Brett (2021) 'Post-millennial Local Whiteness: Racialism, White Dis/advantage and the Denial of Racism', *Ethnic and Racial Studies* 44, 3: 355–73.

Sunak, Rishi and Rajeswaran, Saratha (2014) *A Portrait of Modern Britain*. London: Policy Exchange.

Szatan, Gabriel (2021) 'Winning Team, Winning Melodies: Euro 2020 and Terrace Anthems', *The Observer* 10 July. www.theguardian.com /football/2021/jul/10/winning-team-winning-melodies-euro-2020 -and-terrace-anthems.

Taguieff, Pierre-André (2001) *The Force of Prejudice: On Racism and Its Doubles*. Minneapolis: University of Minnesota Press.

Thurston, Chloe N. (2018) 'Black Lives Matter, American Political Development, and the Politics of Visibility', *Politics, Groups, and Identities* 6, 1: 162–70.

Tillery, Alvin B. (2019) 'What Kind of Movement Is Black Lives Matter? The View from Twitter', *Journal of Race, Ethnicity, and Politics* 4, 2: 297–323.

Twine, France Winddance and Blee, Kathleen M. (eds.) (2001) *Feminism and Antiracism: International Struggles for Justice*. New York University Press.

University of Bristol (2022) *The University of Bristol: Our History and the Legacies of Slavery*. University of Bristol.

University of Cambridge (2022) *Advisory Group on Legacies of Enslavement: Final Report*. University of Cambridge.

van Dijk, Teun A. (2020) *Antiracist Discourse in Brazil: From Abolition to Affirmative Action*. Lanham: Lexington Books.

van Dijk, Teun A. (2021) *Anti-racist Discourse: Theory and History of a Macromovement*. Cambridge University Press.

Virdee, Satnam (2014) *Racism, Class and the Racialized Outsider*. Basingstoke: Palgrave Macmillan.

Virdee, Satnam, Taylor, Mhairi and Masterton, Cassie (2021) *Understanding Racism, Transforming University Cultures*. University of Glasgow.

Walcott, Rinaldo (2021) *The Long Emancipation: Moving toward Black Freedom*. Durham, NC: Duke University Press.

Walters, Lindsey K. (2017) 'Slavery and the American University: Discourses of Retrospective Justice at Harvard and Brown', *Slavery & Abolition* 38, 4: 719–44.

Warmington, Paul (2024) *Permanent Racism: Race, Class and the Myth of Post-racial Britain*. Bristol: Policy Press.

Warren, Mark R. (2021) *Willful Defiance: The Movement to Dismantle the School-to-Prison Pipeline*. New York: Oxford University Press.

Waters, Rob (2019) *Thinking Black: Britain, 1964–1985*. Oakland: University of California Press.

Waters, Rob (2023) 'Race, Citizenship and "Race Relations" Research in Late-Twentieth-Century Britain', *Twentieth Century British History* 34, 3: 491–514.

Wieviorka, Michel (1995) *The Arena of Racism*. London: SAGE.

Williams, Thomas Chatterton (2010) *Losing My Cool: How a Father's Love and 15,000 Books Beat Hip-hop Culture*. New York: Penguin Press.

Williams, Thomas Chatterton (2019) *Self-Portrait in Black and White: Unlearning Race*. New York: W. W. Norton & Company.

Yancy, George and Bywater, Bill (eds.) (2024) *In Sheep's Clothing: The Idolatry of White Christian Nationalism*. Lanham: Rowman & Littlefield.

Yazici, Edanur, Murji, Karim, Keith, Michael, Pile, Steve, Solomos, John and Wang, Ying (2023) '"London Is Avocado on Toast": The Urban Imaginaries of the #LondonIsOpen Campaign', *Urban Studies* 60, 12: 2418–35.

Zamalin, Alex (2019) *Antiracism: An Introduction*. New York University Press.

Zoellner, Tom (2020) *Island on Fire: The Revolt that Ended Slavery in the British Empire*. Cambridge, MA: Harvard University Press.

Index